TOXIC RELATIONSHIPS

UNDERSTAND THE SIGNS, IDENTIFY MANIPULATION,
SET BOUNDARIES, AND EMPOWER POSITIVE
CHANGE AFTER BREAKING FREE FROM A POISONOUS
PARTNER

TERRI PENDLETON, LMHC

CONTENTS

INTRODUCTION

> *"Healing may not be so much about getting better as about letting go of everything that isn't you – all of the expectations, all of the beliefs – and becoming who you are."*
>
> — RACHEL NAOMI REMEN

Did you know that a staggering 80% of Americans have faced emotional abuse? That number might seem exaggerated, but think about it for a second. As you walk down a bustling street, visit your local coffee shop, or attend a family gathering, nearly 4 out of every 5 people you interact with have, at one point or another, felt the suffocating grip of an emotionally toxic relationship. If you've picked up this book, you're among them.

The heaviness of these relationships isn't confined to the abuser and the abused. They ripple out, creating waves of distress, uncertainty, and tension in every facet of life. From dimming one's spark at work to causing hesitation in forming new connections, these relationships cast long shadows. The aftershocks can even reverberate into stable, loving relationships, seeding doubt and discord.

Feelings of isolation often plague victims of emotional abuse. It's not uncommon to feel adrift, like floating in an endless sea with no land in sight. Friends and family might seem miles away, and though they call out to you, their voices are faint whispers drowned out by the storms of doubt, guilt, and regret. You've probably had moments where you've felt trapped in a cycle, an ever-tightening loop of self-doubt. Every attempt to break free, to gasp for a breath of fresh air, feels like it's met with a stronger gust, pushing you back into the depths.

Yet, it was a specific moment, that catalyst, that final straw that compelled you to seek answers and find refuge. Perhaps it was one of those sleepless nights where tears seemed endless, each droplet a testament to the pain you've been enduring. Or maybe it was an argument, words laced with venom, making you feel small, belittled, and utterly insignificant. The silent longing for a love that nurtures, not degrades, is what brought you here. Deep down, buried beneath layers of denial or apprehension, you're searching for clarity, guidance, and, most importantly, healing—whether you've admitted it to yourself.

Before we embark on this journey of introspection and healing, I want to share a story with you. Two years ago, I had a patient, Lisa. A vibrant woman in her early 30s, Lisa was a picture of success. A high-powered job, accolades under her belt, and friends who adored her. But behind that radiant smile lay a secret she hadn't shared with anyone. Lisa was trapped in a toxic relationship that was gradually eroding her self-worth. On the outside, her life seemed perfect, but internally, she was crumbling. Like you, she had moments of desperation, seeking a lifeline. Her path to healing wasn't straightforward, but it was worth every challenging step.

The perplexing thing about toxic relationships is that they only sometimes start as such. More often than not, they commence with what seems like fairy-tale beginnings. Whirlwind romances, passionate encounters, and promises of forever. The mask, however, gradually starts to slip, revealing a once-hidden facade. Recognizing these patterns and having the tools to deal with them is your first step toward emancipation.

That's precisely what this book aims to provide. You're not merely going to read about the whats and whys of toxic relationships, but you'll also delve into the hows. Identifying these hidden patterns, even when they're masterfully disguised as love or care, and how to rebuild your shattered self-worth and regain the confidence that might have eroded over time. Think of this not just as a book but as a roadmap—a guide leading you away from the emotional chains that have held you back. By the end of our journey together, you'll be armed with the wisdom and strategies to free yourself from past traumas and foster healthier, more fulfilling future relationships.

The most crucial thing I want you to remember is this: you're not alone. The feeling of isolation, that you're the only one enduring such pain, is a common sentiment. But as the stories mentioned earlier, and countless others I've encountered, demonstrate, a vast community has faced, fought, and found its way out of the labyrinth of emotional toxicity.

Imagining life after a toxic relationship might seem like a distant dream. But let me paint you a picture. Imagine waking up, and the first emotion you feel isn't dread or anxiety but hope. Imagine looking into the mirror and seeing not a broken spirit but a resilient soul, ready to face the day. Envision relationships where mutual respect, love, and understanding aren't the exceptions but the norm. A life where your worth isn't determined by another but recognized and celebrated by yourself. That's not a mere fantasy; it's a reality within your grasp.

Why should you trust this book or even the words I write? What makes me a credible guide on this journey? It's not just the three decades I've spent as a licensed mental health counselor, although that has given me ample time to refine my understanding and techniques. It's the countless faces and stories I've seen and heard. From the young woman grappling with her first heartbreak to the middle-aged man coming to terms with years of subtle manipulation, I've witnessed transformations that have both humbled and inspired me.

The mental health field has evolved, and so have I with it. With the rise in societal awareness about mental health, self-care, and the importance of healthy relationships, the tools at our disposal are now more sophisticated and effective. This book embodies cumulative knowledge, ensuring you get age-old wisdom and the latest insights from scientific research and therapy practices.

However, I'll be the first to admit that knowing and healing were two different battles. I remember the struggle before these tools were at our disposal. Those seeking help would often be trapped in trial-and-error cycles, with little more than intuition and blind faith to guide them. Those days were tough; seeing the pain and confusion on their faces was heart-wrenching. The progress was slow, and the path to recovery was often riddled with setbacks. The absence of a comprehensive guide made the journey more treacherous than it needed to be.

That's where this book comes in. Think of it as the bridge that spans the tumultuous waters of toxic relationships, leading you safely to the other side. I've put together this guide with the earnest hope that no one else has to face the daunting challenge of navigating these waters without a sturdy support system.

But here's a little secret, one that might surprise you. The power to change, heal, and create a brighter future isn't just in this book. It's within you. Hidden beneath the layers of pain, doubt, and fear is a strength you might have forgotten but is very much alive. A resilient spirit ready to claim its rightful place in the world.

It's okay if you're not ready to believe that just yet. Remember, healing is a journey, not a destination. As you flip through these pages, let the words be your companion, a gentle reminder that love in its purest form awaits amidst the chaos. A love that sees, hears, and values you. A love that doesn't judge. The longing you've kept hidden, even from yourself, is not just a desire but a destiny waiting to be fulfilled.

Clients often say, "I wish I had found this information sooner." Remember, there is always time to start anew. You're here now, taking the first steps toward a future with possibilities. Embrace this moment, for it marks the beginning of a transformative journey. And as you journey forward, remember, every page turned, every insight gained is a step closer to the life you've always deserved.

1

DIVING INTO MURKY WATERS

"Sometimes, it takes a heartbreak to shake us awake and help us see we are worth so much more than we're settling for."

— MANDY HALE

Decades in this profession have acquainted me with countless tales of heartache and triumph, like the story of Heather and Derek, which I often recount to clients grappling with the shadows of a toxic relationship.

Heather and Derek appeared to have it all. From the outside, their love story was the stuff of fairy tales.

High school sweethearts, they held hands through the maze of life, from college challenges to career transitions. Their Facebook posts were replete with pictures of candlelit dinners and romantic getaways, eliciting a wave of *'#CoupleGoals'* comments. But behind those filtered photos was an entirely different story.

Heather tearfully confided about the growing chasm in their relationship. Derek, once her pillar of strength, had begun undermining her subtly yet consistently. It started innocuously enough — slight jabs at her appearance or playful mockery of her aspirations. But soon, the playful banter masked hurtful taunts, and his 'protectiveness' veered into possessiveness.

The root of many toxic relationships is not explosive fights or overt abuse. Instead, it's the insidious, constant erosion of self-worth. Heather began questioning her judgment, her appearance, and even her very essence. Yet, the weight of societal expectations, the fear of judgment, and her tangled emotions kept her anchored.

Many of you might recognize shades of Heather's story in your own lives. The cultural tapestries we come from often value familial harmony over individual well-being, making it even harder to acknowledge the toxicity lurking in our relationships.

Toxic doesn't always mean dramatic showdowns. Sometimes, it's the simmering undertone of disrespect. Sometimes, it's the gnawing feeling that your dreams and emotions are continually sidelined. Often, it's the realization that the love you once felt has been replaced by fear — fear of loneliness or the unknown future without your partner.

But here's the ray of sunshine in this gloomy narrative: recognizing the problem is half the battle won. You've taken the first courageous step toward understanding and healing by picking up this book and delving into this chapter.

Now, I won't tell you to "just leave." I've been around long enough to know life isn't that black and white. But what I will do is guide you through understanding these murky waters. Together, we'll explore the intricate nuances of toxic relationships, offering insights drawn from real-life experiences and scientific research.

Remember, the longing for unconditional love, respect, and understanding is inherent to all of us. And while the path ahead might be challenging, believe that you deserve a relationship where you are seen, heard, and valued without judgment.

While relationships are inherently complex, understanding the distinction between the standard challenges couples face and the signs of a genuinely toxic relationship is critical.

First, let's clarify what we mean by a "toxic relationship." While all relationships experience rough patches, a toxic relationship is characterized by persistent and harmful behaviors that degrade one's self-worth and well-being. As Dr. Lillian Glass, who coined the term, explains, *"Any relationship between people who don't support each other, where there's conflict, and one seeks to undermine the other, is toxic."*

Toxic relationships aren't limited to just romantic partnerships; they can manifest in friendships, familial ties, and even professional settings. However, for our discussion, I'll primarily focus on romantic relationships, drawing from real-life scenarios I've encountered.

EXAMPLES OF TOXIC TRAITS

Navigating relationships requires us to be vigilant, especially when identifying patterns that can harm us emotionally and mentally. While some red flags are glaring, others are more insidious, creeping into our lives almost unnoticed until the damage is profound.

Let's shed light on some of these toxic traits, from the ones that silently gnaw at our self-worth to the overt ones that cannot be ignored.

1. **Constant Criticism:** A partner continuously finds faults, often over inconsequential matters. For instance, Jane tearfully described how her partner ridiculed her cooking, clothing choices, and even her laugh, making her doubt her worth.

2. **Manipulation:** Manipulators sometimes use subtle tactics to control and dominate their partners. For example, a partner might give the silent treatment until their demands are met or make their significant other feel guilty for spending time with friends.

3. **Jealousy and Possessiveness:** While occasional jealousy is natural, extreme possessiveness is not. Partners who constantly question your whereabouts, check your phone, or isolate you from loved ones are displaying toxic behavior. They may also always accuse you of having an affair.

4. **Lack of Support:** In a healthy relationship, partners uplift each other. In contrast, toxic partners undermine or belittle each other's achievements and dreams. I once counseled a

talented artist who'd given up her passion because her partner dismissed her talents as "childish doodles."

5. **Verbal and Physical Abuse:** This is an overt sign but worth emphasizing. No one should endure name-calling, threats, or physical harm.

6. **Gaslighting:** This involves making someone doubt their feelings or memories. A classic example is when a partner cheats but when confronted, convinces the other that they're being paranoid or "imagining things."

7. **Financial Control:** A partner may limit access to money, scrutinize spending, or prevent the other from working, creating a dependency that can be hard to break, especially when children or significant expenses are involved.

8. **Walking on Eggshells:** If you consistently fear your partner's reactions and alter your behavior to avoid conflict, it's a sign of toxicity.

Now, it's essential to understand that every relationship has moments of discord. Disagreements over finances or parenting styles, for example, are standard. But when these disagreements are characterized by consistent disrespect, manipulation, or harm, they cross into toxic territory.

While I wish to sit across from you and discuss your unique circumstances, I can offer these insights. If any of the toxic traits mentioned resonate with your current relationship, take a moment to reflect. Remember, you deserve a relationship filled with respect, love, and mutual growth. Embracing this truth is the first step to navigating these murky waters and making choices aligned with your well-being.

In my experience, I've realized that recognizing the signs of a toxic relationship can often be as elusive as smoke. Sometimes, it's glaringly obvious, and at other times, it's subtle, almost like a whisper in the wind.

FROM WHISPERS TO ROARS: RECOGNIZING THE SIGNS

- **Emotional Exhaustion:** Think of a time when you've had a particularly grueling day. Now, imagine feeling like that every day because of your relationship. If being around your partner constantly leaves you drained, it's a significant red flag.
- **Treading on Eggshells:** Emily said she felt like she was "dancing on a minefield" around her partner. Every conversation had the potential to explode. If this sounds familiar, take note.

- **Constant Criticism:** Remember our chat about toxic traits? A hallmark of toxicity is the unending barrage of criticisms. It's one thing for a partner to point out a stray hair occasionally; it's another to criticize your essence constantly.
- **Control Issues:** Excessive control is stifling and harmful, whether dictating your wardrobe or determining whom you can meet. Love should be freeing, not imprisoning.
- **Erosion of Self-esteem:** Do you question your worth or doubt your decisions more than before? A relationship should uplift, not undercut, your confidence.
- **You're Always the "Villain":** In a toxic relationship, it often feels like you can do no right. Every problem or disagreement is somehow twisted to be your fault.
- **Isolation:** Do you find your social circle shrinking? It could be because your partner is subtly (or not so subtly) pulling you away from friends and family, trying to become the only voice in your life.
- **The Dreaded Gut Feeling:** Intuition is a powerful thing. If something deep down tells you things aren't right, it's worth a closer look. We get that gut feeling or "red flag" and think

we can help them change to be better or love them even more.

- **The Emotional Roller Coaster:** An unpredictable relationship, with intense highs and crushing lows, can be intoxicating but ultimately destructive. Stability is undervalued and essential.
- **Boundary Violations:** A partner who consistently oversteps or dismisses your boundaries isn't respecting you. Remember when you confidently told your partner something, only to find out they'd blurted it out to their friends? That sense of betrayal is painful.

As someone who has seen countless individuals wrestle with the anguish of toxic relationships, I urge you to be vigilant and prioritize your well-being. Don't diminish your feelings or second-guess yourself. While every relationship has challenges, it's essential to discern between typical hurdles and signs of something far more sinister.

And while my voice might be confined to these pages, know that you're not alone on this journey. Numerous individuals have navigated these murky waters before, and many have found their way to clearer shores. If they can, so can you.

After discussing the signs to look out for, getting more granular and discussing the behaviors that make a relationship toxic is crucial. These behaviors are like the pathogens in murky water—nearly invisible but harmful nonetheless.

- **Manipulation:** A manipulative partner knows which strings to pull to make you dance to their tune. They might use guilt, anger, or even affection as tactics to steer you where they want you to go. It's a sneaky move that leaves you questioning your thoughts and decisions.

- **Gaslighting:** Imagine someone subtly altering your reality and then acting like you're losing it. "You're too sensitive" or "Imagining things" are classic lines. It's a tactic that makes you second-guess your own experiences and memories. Let me tell you, as someone who has seen this firsthand with clients, this is one of the most corrosive behaviors you can encounter.

- **Emotional Blackmail:** You're finally ready to put your foot down on something bothering you. But before you can blink, your partner pulls the ultimate guilt trip. They might use phrases like, "If you loved me, you'd do this," holding your emotions hostage. It's a manipulative tactic that directly affects your feelings of love and loyalty.

- **Passive-Aggression:** A passive-aggressive partner will never confront you directly but will find a thousand ways to show their displeasure. Whether it's the silent treatment or sarcastic remarks, they're experts in making you feel bad without overtly saying anything.
- **Financial Abuse:** While we're on the topic, let's not overlook the financial aspect. Many of you have jobs but may find yourselves financially entangled in a way that gives your partner undue power. They might control the purse strings, belittle your earning abilities, or make you feel financially inadequate.
- **Deflecting and Blaming:** Have you ever tried to address an issue and found yourself blamed for causing it in the first place? That's deflecting. It's like trying to nail jelly to a wall; you can't pin these folks down to take responsibility for anything.
- **Physical Aggression:** I would be remiss if I didn't touch on this. Physical abuse is a blatant sign of a toxic, unequivocally unacceptable relationship. At the same time, some may argue that it's "just a one-time thing," once is more than enough to signify a deep-rooted issue.

- **Isolation from Loved Ones:** I've observed a recurring theme in toxic relationships: isolation. Your partner might subtly, or sometimes not so subtly, discourage you from spending time with friends or family. Their reasoning might sound innocent—"They don't understand our love," or "You don't need them when you have me." But it's a tactic to cut you off from your support system, making you more dependent on them.

- **Invasion of Privacy:** Now, let me share a story about Paul. He became frustrated about his partner rifling through his personal belongings, emails, and texts—even tracking his online activity. He felt like a caged bird, unable to have any personal space. If you ever justify your partner's invasion of your privacy, thinking, "It's okay because I have nothing to hide," take a moment to reconsider. Trust is foundational; without it, the relationship can become a prison.

- **Stonewalling:** Nothing more frustrating than being met with a wall when trying to communicate. Instead of addressing issues, the partner might shut down, walk away, or refuse to engage in conversation. It's a tactic to maintain control and avoid taking responsibility.

- **Constant Criticism:** No one's perfect. We all have our quirks. But in a toxic relationship, these quirks become endless points of criticism. It might start with "constructive" advice but can escalate to undermining your self-worth. In time, you might even begin to believe these negative remarks.
- **Jealousy and Possessiveness:** It's natural to feel a tinge of jealousy now and then. But when it spirals into possessiveness, it's a red flag. An overly jealous partner isn't just protective; they're trying to control who you associate with and even the time you spend apart.
- **Ignoring Boundaries:** Healthy relationships respect boundaries. But in a toxic setup, your limitations are repeatedly crossed. Whether it's emotional, physical, or sexual boundaries, a partner's refusal to recognize and respect them is a significant warning sign.

I had a client named Sarah who was in a relationship where nearly all these behaviors were at play. Like many of you, Sarah was a rockstar in her job but felt paralyzed emotionally due to her partner's manipulative behaviors. The complexity and the weight of societal norms kept her tethered. But recognizing these toxic behaviors was her first step towards reclaiming her life.

If you're nodding your head as you read this, don't ignore that gut feeling. You're not overly sensitive, imagining things, or demanding too much. You're simply craving what we all desire—a healthy, respectful, and loving relationship.

Remember, the first step to cleansing the murkiness in your life is to identify what's muddying the waters. It might be challenging, but believe me, it's worth it.

Navigating the complexities of a relationship can feel like walking through a maze blindfolded. But by identifying these behaviors, you're already arming yourself with the tools to find the exit.

Remember, love shouldn't be about control, manipulation, or constant compromise of your well-being. It's about mutual respect, understanding, and growth. And while it's easy for me to write this and for you to read, genuinely internalizing and acting upon it is the real challenge.

Now that we have acquainted ourselves with some intriguing, albeit troublesome, characters that often emerge in toxic relationships, you've probably nodded your head a few times, recognizing one or two of these archetypes in people you know. No judgment here; we've all found ourselves entangled in complexities we never signed up for. But knowing is half the battle, as they say. Let's take a look at the five types of toxic individuals for better clarity:

- If you find yourself drawn to **The Charmer**, be cautious. Charming people can bring joy and excitement, but remember, it's easy to mistake attention for affection. Genuine love goes beyond surface-level charm. If your partner's "loving" gestures start to feel like transactions rather than expressions of affection, it's time to reevaluate.

- As for **The Bully**, it's important to remember that you're not a doormat. I've seen the emotional scars left by bullies often run more profound than any physical ones. Love should never require you to shrink yourself or to live in fear. If you're constantly on high alert, consider seriously if this relationship is worth your peace of mind.

- Listen up for those dealing with **The Mindmixer**: your feelings are valid. If someone makes you question your sanity, you should question their presence in your life. From our previous discussion, Sarah took a while to trust herself again. That's the power these Mindmixers wield—they can make you distrust your inner compass. But remember, self-doubt is the tool they use to keep you tethered. Don't let them.

- **The Taker** loves the spotlight but gives nothing back. Have you ever felt drained, like you're a supporting actor in someone else's drama? Relationships should feel more like a team effort than a solo performance. I've helped numerous clients who were emotionally depleted by their Taker partners. A relationship should replenish you, not leave you running on empty.

- Lastly, **The Keeper** may give you a false sense of security. They promise a world where you and them are the only two people who matter. But that's not love; it's a prison with gilded bars. If your Keeper makes you cut off your support system, consider this: They're not trying to keep you safe; they're trying to keep you to themselves.

So, as we continue to explore these muddy waters, remember that you deserve more than merely to tread water—you deserve to swim freely and joyously.

Now that we've unpacked the five types of toxic individuals you might encounter in relationships, we must distinguish between poisonous relationships and abusive ones. Trust me, this is a nuanced conversation worth having.

The difference might seem subtle, but it's as glaring as a lighthouse in a dark sea when you're living it. Toxic relationships usually feature recurring unhealthy behavior patterns, which may not necessarily be intentionally harmful. The Charmer, The Bully, The Mindmixer—each has their brand of toxicity, but it's not always coming from wanting to hurt you. Sometimes, these people are just as lost in their fog of emotional immaturity.

In contrast, abusive relationships involve patterns of behaviors used to maintain power and control over someone. It's calculated. Whether physical, emotional, or sexual, the abuse is a strategy to dominate. That's a bitter pill, but it's essential to call a spade a spade. Sometimes, the lines blur; for instance, a Mindmixer could escalate into emotional abuse if they start using gaslighting as a tool for control.

What they both have in common, though, is they make you feel less than, like you're not worthy of love, respect, or even basic kindness. Whether it's Jane, a high-powered executive whose partner belittles her career achievements to make himself feel better, or Steve, whose wife manipulates him emotionally to maintain control over family decisions—they all share that sinking feeling of being trapped.

I've had religious and non-religious clients find solace in their beliefs or scientific rationality, thinking that would save their relationships. Neither a higher power nor a Ph.D. in psychology can wave a magic wand and make it all disappear. I wish it were that simple.

Both toxic and abusive relationships can wreak havoc on your mental health and overall well-being. They can seep into other areas of your life, affecting your work performance, relationships with family and friends, and sense of self. Plus, let's not forget the societal pressure to stay in these relationships, sometimes amplified by cultural or religious norms. I get it; you might be stuck between a rock and a hard place, yearning for that unconditional love and respect that seems just out of reach.

I'm sure the advice you're tired of hearing from family and friends is, "Just leave." That won't be peddled here. That's as useful as a screen door on a submarine. We're going to delve into the nitty-gritty, the uncomfortable corners where you've tucked away your fears, your insecurities, and, yes, your hopes.

THE EMOTIONAL AND PHYSICAL TOLL

After we've understood the nature of toxic relationships, we must delve into the consequences they bring into our lives. It's not merely about those gut-wrenching feelings of tension when you step into your home or that mild nausea whenever your phone buzzes. It's much more profound.

A growing feeling of worthlessness is at the heart of these relationships' emotional turmoil. Can you remember a time when you felt you weren't enough? I recall a patient from a few years back, a bright-eyed young woman who had accomplished so much yet believed she was never good enough because her partner, under the guise of "just joking," constantly belittled her. These seeds of self-doubt, once sown, lead to a garden of constant anxiety. You become the ever-watchful gardener, always on edge, expecting the next jibe, the following snide remark, even when they aren't there.

And as days turn to months and months to years, the emotional toll slowly morphs into more severe mental health concerns. It's like that slow drip in your bathroom faucet you never bothered to fix, and over time, the constant dripping wears away at the sink, corroding it. The mind isn't much different. Prolonged exposure to toxicity can potentially usher in anxiety disorders, setting the stage for depressive episodes. There are days when getting out of bed feels like scaling Mount Everest, and sometimes, even the simplest tasks seem impossible.

It doesn't stop there. Sometimes, when the toxicity involves more overt or covert forms of manipulation and betrayal, you might experience symptoms similar to PTSD. Flashbacks, nightmares, an overwhelming sense of fear – I've seen strong individuals crumble under its weight. Like Ben, a middle-aged teacher who experienced panic attacks whenever he heard a car similar to his ex's pull up. His ex would do surprise 'drop-ins' to keep tabs on him.

Toxicity in relationships doesn't discriminate whether you're a high-flying executive or a homemaker. Your background, job, or financial situation doesn't provide immunity. Maria, a financial analyst, once confessed to me her struggle with focusing on her work, her thoughts imprisoned by her partner's previous night's tirade.

While the increasing societal dialogue on mental health and self-care offers a glimmer of hope, the journey isn't linear. You might take two steps forward and then, a memory, a song, a scent, and you're three steps back.

But remember, it's a journey, not a sprint. Each step, however small, is progress.

While the scars left by such relationships run deep, healing is possible. It's a dance of recognizing the pain, understanding its roots, and taking active healing steps.

It's a sunlit Sunday morning. Imagine sitting by the window, your favorite mug of coffee warming your hands. A gentle breeze flits in, and all seems well with the world. But then your heart suddenly races, your palms feel clammy, and a dull ache forms behind your eyes. What's happening? You've had a restful night. Why this sudden feeling of being unwell?

Our bodies have a sneaky way of mirroring the chaos within our minds, especially in our relationships. And sometimes, the physical manifestations of a toxic relationship can be just as damaging, if not more so, than the emotional ones.

I've met countless people who've worn their pain on the inside, hidden beneath layers of "I'm fine" and masked smiles. But sooner or later, the body speaks up, and it's essential to listen.

An ever-increasing heart rate isn't just about nerves or jitters. In continuous emotional stress, our bodies produce excess cortisol – that pesky stress hormone. Over time, this can lead to higher blood sugar levels. It's as if your body's internal thermostat is always set to 'high alert.' And while a little bit of stress can be good – think of that adrenaline rush before a big presentation – the constant stress from toxicity can skyrocket your blood pressure.

Ever heard of the saying, "dying of a broken heart"? It's not just poetic. The stress and anxiety from toxic relationships and increased blood pressure and sugar levels can significantly strain our hearts, increasing the risk of heart problems.

Susan, a vibrant woman in her 40s, once shared how her toxic relationship had left her grappling with unexplained fatigue. Her heart felt heavy, not just metaphorically but physically, too. Medical tests later revealed that the persistent stress had begun to take a toll on her heart's health.

Now, I'm not saying every headache or fatigue directly results from a toxic relationship. Still, it's crucial to recognize when our body is constantly trying to wave a red flag. When your body speaks, it urges you to reflect on what's causing this upheaval.

While mental scars can often be masked, the body's reactions are tangible and concrete. They serve as stark reminders of the impact of toxicity. And while we might pour our energy into our jobs, families, and passions, remember this: No ambition, societal expectation, or perceived obligation is worth sacrificing our well-being.

Like unwelcome guests, toxic relationships might overstay, but it's our home, our sanctuary. And it's time we reclaimed our mental and physical space. So the next time your heart races too fast or that headache persists, take a moment. Breathe. Reflect. Your body is telling a story.

Years ago, I chatted with a dear friend over a cup of chai. We both loved the light spiciness of it, the way it warmed us from the inside. Mid-conversation, she abruptly set her cup down, stared at her trembling hands, and whispered, "Is it strange that my body feels like it's betraying me?"

Toxic relationships have an insidious way of creeping into our psyche. The wounds are often invisible, hidden beneath layers of rationalization and denial, making them harder to recognize. Just like my friend's trembling hands, our bodies show signs. Sometimes, they whisper and scream, but they always reveal the truth about the emotional chaos within.

RECOGNIZING THE TELLTALE SIGNS

Understanding our own well-being isn't always just about introspection; sometimes, it's about interpreting the signals our bodies send us. As we delve into the subtler signs that might hint at the strain of a toxic relationship, we'll see how the emotional tumult manifests physically. Let's dive into some of these telltale signs your body might be revealing:

- **Persistent Fatigue**: It's not just about the occasional lack of sleep. It's a weariness that seeps into your bones, making even simple tasks seem Herculean.
- **Sleep Disturbances**: Finding yourself either sleeping too much or battling insomnia? Your relationship might be the unexpected culprit.
- **Frequent Headaches or Migraines**: Constant stress can lead to tension in the neck and head, leading to painful headaches.
- **Stomach Issues**: Have you ever had butterflies when you're nervous? Now, imagine that feeling, but it's angry hornets instead, causing stomach aches, nausea, or even loss of appetite.
- **Increased Heart Rate and Blood Pressure**: A body constantly on "high alert" can lead to these physical manifestations.

- **Unexplained Aches & Pains**: Sometimes, the emotional pain gets translated into physical discomfort in various body parts.
- **Compromised Immunity**: Falling sick more often? Chronic stress weakens the immune system, making you more susceptible to illnesses.
- **Changes in Weight**: Significant weight changes could be a sign, whether it's weight gain due to emotional eating or weight loss due to loss of appetite.

I want you to pause and reflect if you recognize several of these symptoms. Sometimes, our bodies understand things before our hearts and minds do. And it's high time we pay attention.

Remember that chat over chai? My friend eventually sought therapy and understood that her body's reactions were linked to her toxic relationship. She worked on rebuilding her life, and today, she's thriving. She often tells me, "I wish I had listened to my body sooner."

It's easy to dismiss these signs, especially when we're conditioned to believe that "love conquers all." Love should never come at the cost of your health and well-being. Over the years, I've seen countless people bravely confront their pain, and you can too. Start by listening to the story your body is trying to tell. Remember, it's never just about the chai. It's about understanding what makes your hands tremble when holding that cup.

TEARS IN THE RAIN: JENNIFER'S STORY

Jennifer is a 32-year-old retail manager. She had this poetic way of describing her feelings. She'd say, "It feels like crying in the rain, where my tears blend with the droplets, and no one knows the difference." You see, Jennifer was a sensitive soul who felt things deeply and embraced the world with an open heart. Sometimes, having an open heart means getting hurt much easier.

Jennifer's partner, Adam, often saw her sensitivity as a sign of weakness. Instead of embracing it, he chose to mock it. Every tear shed allowed him to label her a "crybaby." It's heartbreaking. To have the core of your being ridiculed by the one who's supposed to stand by you.

Jennifer's story is familiar. Many of us find ourselves in relationships where our essence is continuously chipped away, bit by bit, until we're mere shadows of who we once were. And like Jennifer, we start hiding those parts of ourselves, stifling our feelings, pushing our tears to the corners of our eyes until we can release them in private.

But there's an inherent danger in this. By hiding her emotions, Jennifer told herself her feelings weren't valid. It's akin to clipping the wings of a bird and then asking it why it doesn't fly. Over time, this erodes our self-worth, making us question our reality, feelings, and sanity.

I asked Jennifer, "When did you feel safe expressing your emotions around Adam?" She paused, reflecting, and then, with a sigh, said, "I can't remember." That's the thing about toxic relationships; they subtly make you forget who you were before the toxicity seeped in.

Now, I'd like to pause and ask you some questions:

1. Have you ever felt you needed to hide your true feelings from your partner?
2. Do you often second-guess your emotions or consider them "too much"?
3. Can you recall the last time you genuinely felt heard and understood in your relationship?

Your answers to these questions shine a light on areas of your relationship that need attention. Everyone, including Jennifer, deserves a relationship where they feel seen, heard, and, most importantly, understood. With the right tools, awareness, and support, we can transform our relationships or find the strength to seek better ones.

As our sessions continued, Jennifer started to reclaim her voice, setting boundaries and reminding herself daily of her worth. She realized she wasn't a "*crybaby.*" She was human, deserving of respect and understanding. And so are you. Remember, your feelings are valid, and you should never have to cry in the rain to hide them.

In our journey together through these pages, it's crucial to understand that toxic relationships often don't come with blazing warning signs or flashing neon lights. Instead, they can be insidious, sneaking up on us like a cloud slowly covering the sun. Before we realize it, our once sunny and cheerful lives become overcast with doubt, mistrust, and feelings of inadequacy.

I've seen that it's often not the overt actions but the subtle, nuanced signs that cause the most harm. Like a constant drip on a stone, these subtle behaviors can erode even the most robust self-esteem. The sarcastic remarks disguised as jokes, the offhand comments that make you question your worth, or the seemingly innocent neglect that makes you feel invisible. These signs often go unnoticed, brushed under the rug, and rationalized as "not that bad."

Jennifer's story is just one of the many tales echoed in my office. Her tears in the rain symbolize the silent cries of countless souls trapped in toxic relationships, struggling to find their voice.

In our upcoming chapter, we'll delve deeper into these nuanced signs. We'll learn to identify them, understand their impact, and, most importantly, equip ourselves with strategies to navigate and address them. Remember, knowledge is power, and by understanding these hidden signs, we can better protect our hearts, minds, and souls from the damaging effects of toxic relationships. Remember, while the rain might hide your tears today, you can return to clearer skies and brighter days with the proper guidance.

2

READING BETWEEN THE LINES

"Sometimes it takes leaving to truly understand what you were under. It's a feeling, an emotion, an energy... that can spare your life or kill you. Recognize it. Remove it."

— R.H. SIN

O ne universal truth still stands: Recognizing toxicity is the first step to healing from it. This chapter is about the silent alarms, the seemingly inconspicuous signs that hint at something amiss in your relationship. My patients have often sat across from me, tears spilling down their faces, confessing, "I just didn't see it coming." But upon further reflection, they almost always had. They'd seen the red flags but misunderstood or, even more tragically, ignored them.

I remember when a young woman confided in me about how she'd find herself involuntarily holding her breath whenever her partner walked into the room as if bracing for something. It wasn't fear of physical violence but rather an anticipation of subtle jabs, snide remarks, or cold indifference. This involuntary reaction of her body was its way of saying, "This isn't right." But she'd brushed it off, thinking she was just being "too sensitive."

As we journey through this chapter, let's learn to decipher these understated cues. Let's understand what they're trying to tell us about our environment and the people we surround ourselves with. Your gut instinct and the knowledge you'll gain here can be the guiding light you've been searching for.

SPOTTING THE SILENT ALARMS

In my years as a psychotherapist, I've noticed a particular pattern many people fall into when they're in toxic relationships. They've developed an internal compass, subconsciously guiding them around their partner's moods and triggers. It's a coping mechanism. However, these 'adaptations' can harm their well-being and are like silent sirens signaling a deeper issue. These are the silent alarms that are often overlooked or dismissed. Shall we explore them a bit more?

1. **Small Behavioral Changes**: Think about the times you laughed without restraint or danced without a care. If you notice you're holding back your true self, it might be time to ask yourself why.

2. **Hesitation in Conversations**: I recall a patient who once mentioned rehearsing her sentences in her mind before speaking to her partner. Not for eloquence but for fear. Sound familiar?

3. **Avoidance of Certain Topics**: It's a clear sign when certain subjects become 'no-go' zones, like walking on eggshells navigating around areas that could crack.

4. **Reluctance to Share Feelings**: Your emotions are your north star. If you are stifling tears, joys, or fears, ask yourself why these feelings aren't finding a voice.

5. **Predicting Their Reactions Becomes Second Nature**: Do you plan events, dinners, or casual chats based on how your partner might react?

6. **Your Achievements Become Whispered Celebrations**: Hesitating to share your

triumphs because they might be belittled?
That's an alarm bell.

7. **Constant Vigilance is Your Default Mode**:
One client described feeling like a sentry in his
home, bracing for the next unexpected
skirmish. If this resonates, it's time for some
reflection.

8. **A Sudden Cloud of Anxiety or Depression**:
Your emotions often mirror your surroundings.
If interactions with your partner often leave
you feeling drained or anxious, it's something
to consider deeply.

Understanding relationships can be like navigating a
maze. Yet, these silent alarms are the echoes from
within, telling you something needs attention. Listen to
them. Reflect. And most importantly, trust in yourself
and your feelings.

THE CONCEPT OF MICROAGGRESSIONS WITHIN INTIMATE RELATIONSHIPS

In our journey to understand the intricate threads of
toxic relationships, a subtle but piercing concept often
escapes notice: microaggressions. Having sat across
from countless individuals, I've heard them articulate
experiences that, while seeming minor in isolation,

when stacked together, create an insurmountable weight on their hearts and minds.

Now, you might be wondering, "What exactly are microaggressions?" They are brief, everyday interactions that subtly, and often unintentionally, communicate hostile or discriminatory attitudes towards a person. In intimate relationships, these microaggressions often mask more profound issues of power, control, and disrespect. They can be verbal, non-verbal, or even in the form of a slight.

Allow me to illustrate with a few examples:

1. **"You're overreacting."** It's a phrase I've heard so many recounts. While it may seem harmless, it invalidates the other person's emotions and experiences.
2. **Forgetting important dates repeatedly**: It's human to forget once in a while, but when it becomes a pattern, it might signal a lack of consideration or even passive aggression.
3. **Jokes that sting**: We all love a bit of humor, but when your partner makes 'jokes' that touch on your insecurities or belittle you, that's a red flag.
4. **Comparing you with others**: "Why can't you be more like [insert name]?" Ever heard that one? It's a subtle way of eroding self-worth.

5. **Ignoring or avoiding**: The silent treatment or acting as if you're invisible can be deeply hurtful, even if no words are exchanged.

A few years back, I had a young woman in my office, teary-eyed, recounting how her partner often dismissed her career achievements with comments like, "Must be easy being in a field dominated by women." On the surface, this might seem like a mere observation, but beneath lay layers of belittlement and disregard.

It's crucial to understand that the hurt from microaggressions often accumulates over time, much like a paper cut. One might not seem like much, but many can leave you feeling wounded over time.

If you're nodding along thinking, "This sounds familiar," remember that recognizing these patterns is the first step towards addressing them. While not all microaggressions are intentional or malicious, they reflect deeper dynamics in the relationship that deserve attention. The heart of the matter is mutual respect, understanding, and compassion. If these are lacking, it's time for introspection and dialogue.

Always value yourself and your well-being. Trust your feelings. Know that you deserve a relationship where you feel seen, heard, and valued—without the sting of these subtle yet profound aggressions.

THE IMPORTANCE OF EMOTIONAL INTELLIGENCE AND ACTIVE LISTENING IN IDENTIFYING THESE QUIET INDICATORS

In our last conversation, we navigated the shadowy alleys of microaggressions. It's crucial to expand on how to identify these subtle forms of toxicity. And for that, we'll need to dive into two essential skills— emotional intelligence and active listening. Trust me, these aren't just buzzwords; they're your personal GPS in the maze of complex relationships.

Let's start with emotional intelligence. It's that amazing skill you never knew you needed until life hits you with a dilemma wrapped in layers of mixed signals. What does it do? Simply put, emotional intelligence enables you to understand, interpret, and manage emotions, both your own and those of others. Think of it like your inner emotional detective; it helps you pick up clues, even when they're not handed over in an envelope.

When you're emotionally intelligent, you're not just hearing words but reading between the lines. Remember that time when your partner muttered, "Fine," but the energy in the room dropped ten degrees? Emotional intelligence helps you gauge that, pushing you to dig deeper. You could carry on without it, blind to the storm brewing in your relationship.

Now, onto active listening, the second pillar. This isn't the "Uh-huh, go on" kind of listening while scrolling through Instagram. Active listening is being fully present—mind, body, and soul. It's about showing empathy, asking clarifying questions, and avoiding jumping to conclusions. If emotional intelligence is your inner detective, consider active listening as the flashlight it uses to comb through the dark.

When I started my career, a couple came into my office on the brink of separation. The wife felt unheard, and the husband felt misunderstood. Both were good people, but they'd become so absorbed in their own narratives that they'd forgotten how to listen—really listen—to each other. They had low emotional intelligence and weaker listening skills. Fast forward six months and some intensive therapy, their relationship was transformed. They learned to listen, not just to reply, but to understand. And that made all the difference.

So, why are these skills especially crucial for spotting silent alarms? Well, toxicity isn't always loud and in-your-face. Sometimes, it's in the eye roll your partner gives when you talk about your day or the abrupt topic change when you mention your feelings. These little things speak volumes, and you need emotional intelligence to perceive them and active listening skills to interpret them.

I know you're up against a lot. Your job, maybe kids, societal expectations, and the ever-ticking clock make you feel like you need to have your life sorted yesterday. But honing emotional intelligence and active listening won't just benefit your romantic life; they'll also give you a leg up in every other human interaction you have.

PSYCHOLOGICAL IMPACTS OF IGNORING THESE SILENT ALARMS OVER TIME

So, you're becoming emotionally intelligent and honing your active listening skills—fantastic! But what happens if you turn a blind eye to the silent alarms you're now capable of spotting?

Ignoring a red flag doesn't just make it vanish, as much as we'd like to think it does. And over time, sweeping these issues under the rug can cause stress to accumulate in your emotional bank. Just as a pipe bursts under too much pressure, ignoring these signs can lead to emotional outbursts, debilitating anxiety, and a loss of self-esteem. You'll start questioning your worth and, worse yet, normalize toxicity.

Do you remember that emotional detective we talked about? Imagine if they knew about a crime but chose to look the other way. Eventually, the whole community would suffer, as would the detective's peace of mind. In the same way, your emotional well-being takes a hit when you dismiss your instincts. Trust me, it's far better to confront a problem when it's a molehill rather than a mountain.

A couple of years ago, I worked with a client who had suppressed her feelings and doubts for years. She wanted her marriage to work so badly that she ignored every alarm screaming at her, from her husband's repeated insults to his growing emotional detachment. When she finally came to me, the baggage she carried was unbearable. Her self-esteem was in shambles, and it took years of therapy to rebuild her emotional stability.

Let's remember when you're in a long-term relationship or have children, the consequences multiply. Are those red flags you're ignoring? You're not the only one impacted. Your children are emotional sponges, absorbing every dynamic, whether healthy or unhealthy. You might think you're protecting them by not "rocking the boat," but you're setting a precedent for what they consider normal in relationships.

Now, I know there's societal pressure. Your family may have a 'stay together at all costs' mentality. Or your circle values the picture-perfect couple who "have it all together." These influences can make you dismiss your feelings, making you an accomplice in your emotional neglect. But societal norms should never outweigh your mental health.

Here's the takeaway: don't treat silent alarms like a pesky fly to be swatted away. They're more like an early warning system, a chance to redirect the relationship— or, in some cases, to consider whether the relationship has run its course. We're in a new era that's embracing mental health and self-care, so let's use these tools to build better, healthier connections.

I get it; acknowledging these red flags can be terrifying. It's like opening Pandora's box—you don't know what will happen. But I promise the momentary discomfort of facing these issues is worth the long-term gain. A little turbulence now can save you from a crash landing later on. Your future self will thank you for having the courage to listen, observe, and act.

VERBAL KNIVES: UNMASKING ABUSE

Words are like the double-edged swords of the emotional realm. They have the power to mend the deepest of wounds, but they can also cut sharper than a blade. Understanding this dynamic is essential, especially when caught in the web of verbal abuse.

When we think of abuse, it's easy to visualize physical scars. But let me tell you, over my three decades as a therapist, I've witnessed the profound impact of verbal injuries. Invisible, yet devastating. There's a saying in therapy circles: broken bones heal, but cruel words echo.

I remember a session with a young woman named Karina. She was vibrant, intelligent, and full of life. Yet, with tears in her eyes, she confessed to me how her partner's consistent belittlement had made her feel invisible. "He never hits me," she whispered, "but his words leave marks on my soul."

In toxic relationships, words become weapons. Disguised as 'honest feedback' or 'constructive criticism,' they slowly chip away at one's self-esteem. Manipulative phrases like "You shouldn't feel that way" or "You're totally overreacting" are often thrown around to invalidate the other person's feelings.

There are countless Katrinas out there, questioning their worth and doubting their sanity, all because of the verbal knives thrown their way. The tricky part? Unlike physical abuse, where the harm is evident, verbal abuse is sneaky. It seeps into your consciousness, altering the way you view yourself.

By now, you might be wondering, "Am I in a verbally abusive relationship?" Well, it's not always black and white. What starts as a snide remark here or a sarcastic comment there can snowball into a pattern. Before you know it, these jabs become a part of your daily life. But remember, constant criticism, belittlement, and humiliation are not normal in any relationship.

Recognizing verbal abuse is the first step to healing. But confronting it? That requires courage, support, and understanding. You deserve a relationship where words are a balm, not a weapon. Where you are uplifted, cherished, and valued. Remember, your voice matters, and so do your feelings.

Next time you find yourself on the receiving end of hurtful words, take a step back. Reflect. Do you find this pattern recurring? Are you often left feeling smaller, insignificant, or questioned? If so, it's time to look closer and seek guidance.

The path to healing is challenging, but acknowledging the issue is half the battle won. Always remember: words have power, but so do you.

TYPES OF VERBAL ABUSE

Peeling back the layers of a toxic relationship is like delving into a novel with countless subplots. Verbal abuse, as we discussed earlier, is an unseen wound, one that's often overlooked because of its non-physical nature. I've sat across from countless individuals in my therapy room who've struggled to pinpoint and label their emotional turmoil. I've come to understand that recognizing these patterns is the first step to healing.

Let's delve deeper into the dark alleys of verbal abuse, shall we?

1. Belittling: Ah, this is a classic one. Picture this: You shared a proud achievement with your partner, only to be met with a snarky, "That's it?" or "I've seen better." It's as if they've pricked your shining balloon of self-worth with a pin. Over time, these subtle digs can diminish one's self-confidence. Remember my client Maria? This was her partner's favorite weapon.

2. Shouting: An unexpected outburst can be deeply unsettling. It's not always about the volume—it's about the intent. Shouting is a tool of domination, a way to establish control. It says, "My voice will drown out yours, no matter what."

3. Name-Calling: Names have power. Being called "stupid," "lazy," or worse, can sting. Each cruel epithet embeds itself deeper into one's psyche, shaping how they view themselves. There's no love or constructive criticism here; it's pure degradation.

4. Silent Treatment: Sometimes, the absence of words can be louder than any shout. Ignoring someone, acting as though they're invisible, is a manipulative tactic. It's a psychological power play, making the victim feel they've done something so wrong that they don't even deserve acknowledgment.

Now, here's an anecdote from my own experiences. A few years ago, I had a couple come in for therapy. The husband often used the silent treatment on his wife. Whenever she'd do something he didn't like, he'd ice her out, sometimes for days. He'd told himself he was avoiding conflict. But in reality? He was doling out punishment, making her anxious and desperate for his attention. It's a dance I've seen many times over in verbal abuse.

I wish I could say these are the only types of verbal abuse, but they're just the tip of the iceberg. These patterns often overlap, creating a complex tapestry of emotional harm. Recognizing them in your relationship can be like shining a light into a dark room—it reveals the things that have been lurking in the shadows all along.

I'm not here to judge or tell you what to do. My purpose is to provide you with knowledge, insight, and understanding. With that knowledge, you'll be equipped to make the best choices for your well-being. Remember, everyone deserves respect, love, and to have their voice heard. If these patterns resonate with your relationship, know that you're not alone, and there's help and hope ahead.

EXPERT ADVICE ON COPING MECHANISMS AND WAYS TO COUNTERACT THESE FORMS OF ABUSE WITHOUT ESCALATING CONFRONTATIONS

Navigating the choppy waters of a verbally abusive relationship can be like trying to cross a bridge with broken planks. You tread carefully, sometimes back-tracking, and often feeling trapped in a dangerous loop. But, I want to arm you with ways to cope and counteract this form of abuse while ensuring the confrontations don't escalate.

1. **The Power of Reflection:** It's tempting to retaliate when belittled. However, a simple "I hear you" or "I understand you feel that way"

can act as a mirror, reflecting their words back to them. I recall a session with Jasmine, a young woman who felt tormented by her partner's constant jibes. Reflecting on his words made him pause and think, even if momentarily.

2. **Boundaries, Boundaries, Boundaries:** Be assertive but calm. State clearly what is acceptable behavior and what isn't. It's like planting a flag on a mountain peak, signifying that there's a line that shouldn't be crossed. Remember, it's not about picking a fight but laying down the rules.

3. **Disengage, But Not Disconnect:** Think of shouting as a rainstorm. Sometimes, the best thing to do is to find shelter and let it pass. Walk away from the situation, breathe, and return when things are calmer. But this isn't running away; it's a tactical retreat to protect yourself.

4. **Keep a Verbal Abuse Diary:** Documenting instances can serve two purposes. Firstly, it's a record, a stark black-and-white testament to what's occurring. And secondly, as I've often told my clients, writing can be therapeutic. It lets you process emotions; you might discern patterns that help you better anticipate and manage conflicts over time.

5. **Seek Support:** Lean on friends, family, or professional counselors. Sometimes, a listening ear or a shoulder to cry on can be a lifesaver. Jane, a client I saw years back, found solace in a support group. They became her lifeline, providing her strength on days when she felt utterly depleted.

6. **Educate Yourself:** Arm yourself with knowledge. Understand the dynamics of verbal abuse, its origins, and its effects. As the saying goes, "Knowledge is power," the more you understand, the better equipped you are to handle the situation.

7. **Reconnect with Yourself:** Sometimes, amidst the chaos, we lose ourselves. Set aside some 'you time'. Whether it's a hobby, meditation, or just a walk in the park, it's vital to center yourself.

Imagine verbal abuse as an ugly weed in a garden. You don't just pluck it; you get to its roots. These coping mechanisms are your gardening tools. But remember, sometimes, gardens need professional gardeners. Be bold and seek expert advice when things seem over-whelming.

Life's too short, and each one of you is too precious to live under the dark cloud of verbal abuse. While I'm here offering advice from my years of experience, always remember that the power to change your narrative lies within you. I'm just here, holding the torch to light your path.

EMOTIONAL CHAINS AND TRAUMA BOND

I have noticed that sometimes our bonds are not as clear-cut as we'd like them to be. Love, which ideally should feel like a safe harbor, can sometimes feel more like a stormy sea. And those caught in turbulent waters are often held down by what professionals call 'emotional chains' and 'trauma bonds.'

As the term suggests, emotional chains are the invisible ties that bind us to another person. These aren't your regular connections forged out of mutual respect, love, and understanding. No, these chains are knotted together with threads of manipulation, obligation, guilt, and fear.

Now, we dive a little deeper, and we encounter a powerful emotional chain known as a trauma bond. A trauma bond forms between an abuser and the abused. It is an intense emotional connection built on a cycle of highs and lows – abuse followed by apology, pain interspersed with moments of love or what feels like it. The unpredictability of this cycle – never knowing if you'll get tenderness or turmoil – creates a powerful attachment, almost akin to an addiction.

Imagine a pendulum swinging between love and pain. At one end, you have those beautiful moments that remind you of why you fell in love in the first place. And then, it swings to the other extreme, to moments of degradation, hurt, or manipulation. This back-and-forth creates an environment where the abused becomes increasingly dependent on their abuser, constantly yearning for the next "high" in the relationship.

Now, remember Karina from earlier? That shadow over her face, that heaviness in her voice, was her trauma bond speaking. It's that feeling of being "stuck" with someone even when every logical bone in your body screams for you to run. That is the power of these emotional chains. But knowing their name and understanding their nature is the first step in picking the lock and setting yourself free.

While this journey may be challenging, you're not alone. There's strength in knowledge, strength in understanding, and, most importantly, strength within you. Those chains can be broken with time, patience, and professional guidance. Trust me, having witnessed many brave individuals face and overcome these bonds; I know you have it in you to do the same.

HOW TO DEAL WITH TRAUMA BONDING

Knowing you're tethered to a trauma bond can feel like discovering you've been dancing in quicksand. But remember, the realization itself is akin to grabbing a lifeline. As someone privy to the intricate dances of many brave individuals striving to escape this predicament, let me share a roadmap that has helped many:

1. **Empower Through Education**: Think of understanding as your North Star. Immerse yourself in content - through books, documentaries, or insightful TED talks - that enlightens you about trauma bonding. Knowing is like having a compass in a dense forest.

2. **Lay Down the Law**: Setting boundaries and learning to say no is critical. Recognize your limits, set them, and fiercely protect them.

3. **Date Yourself**: Have you ever tried watching a sunset alone or treating yourself to a gourmet meal for one? Now's the time! Rediscover your quirks, passions, and joys. It's a journey of falling in love with oneself.

4. **Guidance Isn't Weakness**: Therapists are like lighthouses, guiding ships safely to harbor. They've been trained to shed light on the

murkiest of emotional waters. So, when in doubt, seek that guiding light.

5. **Build Your Tribe**: I recall a story from my client, Lucas. For him, breaking free from his trauma bond felt like being lost at sea. But when he surrounded himself with a 'crew' of supportive souls, the waves seemed less daunting. So, gather your crew - friends, family, or support groups.

6. **Dance, Walk, or Even Shimmy!** There's an alchemy in movement. It's transformative! A brisk walk, a yoga class, or just dancing like no one's watching can rejuvenate the spirit.

7. **Stay Connected**: While solitude has its moments, cocooning yourself away can amplify negative emotions. A simple conversation, recalling a hilarious incident with a friend, can be the sunshine on a cloudy day.

8. **Pen Down Your Heart**: Remember when we used to write diaries? There's a cathartic power in putting feelings to paper. It gives voice to your innermost thoughts and helps you discern the forest from the trees.

9. **Chart a Fresh Course**: Have you ever dreamt of salsa classes or mastering the art of Italian cooking? Establishing fresh goals and dreams

can reignite the spark of excitement and
purpose in life.

10. **Wrap Yourself in Kindness**: Don't berate
yourself for where you are. Emotions are
intricate tapestries; sometimes, they entangle us
in patterns we didn't envision. Extend the same
kindness to yourself as you would to a dear
friend in a similar situation.

Remember, even after the darkest nights, each dawn
brings fresh hope. Equipped with the proper arsenal of
tools, support, and perseverance, the journey from
entrapment to emancipation becomes feasible and
filled with growth. You have an indomitable spirit; let it
soar!

TWISTED MIRRORS: ANTHONY AND VANESSA'S STORIES

A few years ago, I sat across from Anthony, a brilliant
young man pursuing his master's degree, passionate
about shaping young minds in his classroom. However,
his vivacity was marred by a shadow that haunted him
outside the school's corridors. Anthony's partner,
Justin, routinely hurled demeaning comments at him
like "worthless" and "idiot." Even with the clarity of my
counseling room's ambiance, I saw Anthony's inner

conflict—intellectually, he recognized that Justin's insults reflected his insecurities. Emotions have a way of coloring our lenses, and Anthony started questioning his worth.

He'd say, "There are moments when I wonder if I am as foolish as he claims."

Then there's Vanessa. Oh, Vanessa! She's a beautiful woman in her 60s with a voice that could soothe even the most troubled minds, thanks to her career as a speech therapist. But, a mirror in her home painted a different picture. That mirror witnessed her transformation from a vibrant, joyful spirit to someone barely recognizable—a change that began after she met Ben.

Every day, Ben found new ways to point out Vanessa's supposed 'flaws,' from her cooking to how she dressed. I remember a session when she told me, "He says I can't even wear lipstick right. It's like I've forgotten who I used to be. I look in the mirror, and I see sadness."

Stories like Anthony and Vanessa's aren't unique. Their experiences serve as a poignant reminder that toxic relationships can cast dark clouds over even the brightest individuals. I often refer to the distorted reflections they saw of themselves, primarily influenced by their partners, as 'twisted mirrors.' These mirrors don't show reality; they magnify flaws, imagined or real, drowning out one's true essence.

I've met many Anthonys and Vanessas over the years. And to each of them, I've often said, "You deserve a mirror that reflects your true self, not the version someone else wants you to see."

If you see yourself in Anthony or Vanessa, remember this: Those distorted reflections aren't you. The person you've always been is buried under those misconceptions and doubts. It might take time, support, and a lot of self-love, but you can find that person again. You are so much more than what a twisted mirror shows.

I've had countless conversations with individuals like Anthony and Vanessa. Their stories might differ in the details, but they all revolve around a common theme: the distorted reflection of oneself as shown by a toxic partner.

Firstly, let's delve into Anthony's situation. Here's a bright young man who is molding our children's future and continuing his educational journey. However, his partner's constant negative affirmations are slowly eroding his self-worth. And this is where it gets tricky. Our logical brain knows when something's amiss, but our emotions? They're a different beast altogether.

Have you ever tried arguing with a 3-year-old who's hell-bent on believing the moon is made of cheese? That's how it feels trying to convince our emotional self of something our logical self already knows. Emotions, especially those ingrained over time, are stubborn. They don't just change overnight because our rational mind 'decides' to think differently. And let's be honest, if someone you care about constantly whispers in your ear that you're inadequate, even the sturdiest of us would start to waver.

Years ago, I met a lady who confessed, "I sometimes wonder if I've truly lost my spark or if it's just his words clouding my judgment." Sound familiar?

Vanessa's narrative is similar. She had a radiant spirit that brought warmth to any room she entered. But Ben's constant critiques became the only voice she heard over time. When your partner, who's supposed to uplift you, becomes your harshest critic, it's challenging to recognize the radiant soul staring back from the mirror.

Our self-perception is intricately tied to the feedback we receive from our immediate environment, particularly from those we love and trust. It's a survival mechanism, allowing us to adapt and fit into our social circles. But when the feedback loop gets tainted with toxicity, it's like wearing glasses smeared with dirt. Everything looks distorted.

I remember chuckling with a client once, comparing it to trying to apply lipstick in a foggy bathroom mirror. "You think you're doing a great job," I said, "until you step out and realize it's all over the place!" We had a good laugh, but deep down, we both knew the gravity of our discussion.

So, what's the takeaway here? These 'twisted mirrors,' as I call them, don't truly reflect who you are. The insecurities, biases, and issues of the other person cloud them. The challenge is to clean the mirror, to see ourselves without the fog of someone else's negative perceptions. And while it's not an easy task, trust me when I say it's worth every effort. Underneath that grime is a radiant soul that is waiting to shine.

After sharing the stories of Anthony and Vanessa, it's time for us to take a moment and reflect on our mirrors and our personal journeys. I've always believed that questions have a magical way of shedding light on areas we have yet to give much thought to. Let's go on a little introspective journey together, shall we?

1. **Can You Recall a Moment in Your Life When Someone's Words Distorted Your Self-View?**
   Maybe it was a stray comment from a partner, a

supposed joke from a friend, or criticism from a family member. How did it make you feel, and more importantly, did you begin to see yourself through their lens?

2. **What Kind of Feedback Do You Usually Accept Without Question?** Do you find that you're more susceptible to believing criticism over praise? Why do you think that is? I remember joking with a client about how humans are sometimes like Teflon for compliments but Velcro for insults!

3. **Whose Voice Dominates Your Internal Monologue?** Is it your own, echoing self-affirmations? Or have you unconsciously adopted the voice of a critical ex, a demanding parent, or a judgmental peer?

4. **How Often Do You Clean Your 'Mirror'?** Are you regularly checking in on your self-perception and ensuring that external influences do not tarnish it? What practices can you integrate into your daily routine to maintain clarity?

5. **If You Were to Describe Yourself Through Your Own Eyes, Free From External Influences, What Would That Description Look Like?** This might be challenging, but I encourage you to be genuine and kind.

Years ago, I was working with a young woman reclaiming her identity after a particularly toxic relationship. She said, "Sometimes, I feel like I'm in an art class, sketching my portrait but using someone else's description of me." Such a powerful visualization, isn't it?

I want you to remember that your self-worth isn't a democracy. Only some get a vote. It's essential to discern whose opinions genuinely matter and whose comments should be taken with a pinch (or maybe a whole handful) of salt.

As we journey through this book together, I hope these questions serve as gentle nudges, encouraging you to peel back the layers, clean off the dust, and truly see the incredible person staring back at you in the mirror. Remember, it's your reflection, and you get to choose the narrative.

As we navigate the maze of Anthony and Vanessa's experiences, it becomes evident that toxicity doesn't always appear with a glaring neon sign. Sometimes, it's much more insidious, creeping into our lives like a fog on an unsuspecting coastal town.

Picture this: I once took a vacation in a quaint coastal village. One morning, I decided to take a stroll along the beach. The sun was out, the sky was clear, and I could see the horizon stretch endlessly before me. But within minutes, a thick mist began to envelop the shore. What was once clear became disoriented and obscured. I struggled to navigate back to my starting point, even though I had only been walking for a short time.

Much like that unexpected fog on the beach, manipulation is disorienting, often creeping in when we least expect it. It distorts our reality, making us question the clear paths we once saw and leading us into places we never intended to tread. It's not just about deceitful actions; it's an emotional and psychological smoke-screen that makes it challenging to trust even our instincts.

I've sat across from countless clients, listening to them describe the thick fog of manipulation they've found themselves lost in. "Why didn't I see it sooner?" they often ask. "Why did I let it get this far?"

The answer isn't straightforward. Manipulation is complex, and its architects are often skilled builders of illusion. It's like trying to spot individual drops of water in that fog. But understanding the essence and the tactics of manipulation is the first step in clearing the air.

Remember, it's okay to feel lost at times, especially when the path becomes foggy. But with understanding, resilience, and a bit of that old therapist's wisdom (courtesy of yours truly), you'll find your way back to clear skies and solid ground. Let's embark on that journey together.

3

THE FOG OF MANIPULATION

"When someone shows you who they are, believe them the first time."

— MAYA ANGELOU

Years into my practice, a story stuck with me. It was a rainy afternoon when Jenna, a young woman in her thirties, entered my office. With a sense of urgency, she began, "Every time I think I see the real him, he changes. It's like chasing a mirage."

Jenna's narrative wasn't unique. Many of my clients have shared similar experiences of feeling trapped in a whirlwind of emotions, caught in the dance of manipulation. The song and dance might be familiar, but identifying the choreographer – manipulation – is where things get murky.

I recall another case decades ago. Samuel, a gentleman in his forties, mentioned, "Every time I feel an ounce of clarity, she finds a way to blur my vision again." Just as he felt he was on solid ground, the rules of the game would change. The love he yearned for would be dangled in front of him like a carrot, only to be snatched away, leaving him forever chasing an ever-moving goalpost.

Jenna and Samuel described the fog of manipulation as a thick mist that makes it almost impossible to see the puppet strings controlling one's emotions, choices, and self-worth. This fog doesn't just appear; it's deliberately cast, designed to obfuscate and disorient.

You see, manipulative partners have mastered the art of illusion. They weave a narrative where they are the saviors and any harm caused is your fault or, worse, unintentional. "If only you hadn't done X, I wouldn't have had to do Y." Sounds familiar?

But here's a truth bomb for you: Love should never feel like a tightrope walk. Even with ups and downs, relationships should offer a sense of security, not a perpetual guessing game.

In this chapter, we will pull back the curtain, illuminating the often-shadowy world of manipulative tactics. By the time we reach the end, you'll be equipped with the knowledge and insight to recognize these strategies and the emotional toll they exact.

PROFILES OF THE PUPPETEER

Manipulation is an art, much like a puppeteer's performance. Behind the curtain, the puppeteer's hands deftly control every move of the puppet, making it dance, jump, or even cry. Unless they strain their eyes, the audience only sees the puppet, not the strings attached. Similarly, in toxic relationships, manipulators act like these puppeteers, pulling unseen strings and leading their partners through a choreographed dance of emotions.

In my years of practice, I've seen these "puppeteers" employ a myriad of tactics. Let's delve into some of them:

1. **Guilt-Tripping:** A classic. Picture Clara, a devoted mother and wife. Whenever she'd contemplate spending an evening with her friends or investing time in her hobbies, her husband would sigh and comment, "Another evening the kids and I have to fend for

ourselves, huh?" He wasn't directly forbidding her, but he pulled those guilt strings tight.

2. **Gaslighting:** Perhaps one of the most insidious forms of manipulation. It's the act of making someone doubt their reality. A client of mine, Tom, once shared how his partner would constantly misplace items and blame him. Over time, Tom began to doubt his memory, wondering if he was forgetful.

3. **Playing the Victim:** Recall Emily from an earlier chapter? Whenever she confronted her partner about his hurtful behavior, he'd suddenly bring up his difficult childhood or stressful job. This diversion tactic made Emily feel guilty for even bringing up her concerns, allowing him to dodge accountability and shift the focus onto his "suffering." The issue at hand was skillfully swept under the rug.

4. **Withholding Affection:** Think of it as emotional ransom. Madison, a vibrant woman in her late twenties, once described how her partner would become distant and cold whenever she voiced her opinions, only returning to his loving self once she backed down.

5. **The Silent Treatment:** This is a form of passive-aggressive punishment. The echoing

silence fills the room, even when the TV is blaring. The refusal to communicate holds the relationship hostage.

6. **Shaming:** It's the art of making one feel lesser. "You're going to wear that? I thought you were trying to lose weight?" Such comments, often masked as 'concern,' slowly chip away at a person's self-esteem.

Recognizing these puppeteer tactics is pivotal. Why? Because once you see the strings, they lose their power. The fog starts to lift. Awareness is your sharpest tool in this endeavor.

I once told a young woman, "You cannot control the actions of others, but you can control how you react to them." Recognizing the patterns of manipulation and understanding their play is your first step towards cutting those strings and dancing to your own rhythm.

THE ONSET OF MANIPULATION

Manipulation is like quicksand. It seems like solid ground at first, perhaps even inviting. You don't realize the danger until you're knee-deep, struggling to free yourself from its engulfing grasp. And the more you resist, the deeper you seem to sink.

Several years ago, a young woman named Krista walked into my office. She was a radiant, ambitious individual with dreams that reached the sky. But over the months, I watched that sparkle dim. She recounted tales of her partner's "protectiveness," how he always knew best, and how she felt she could never measure up. It wasn't until she found herself second-guessing every decision and tiptoeing around conversations that she recognized the chains of manipulation binding her. Krista's story isn't uncommon. Manipulation often enters a relationship on silent feet, unnoticed until it has taken a firm hold.

This covert nature of manipulation is what makes it so sinister. It doesn't announce its arrival with loud proclamations. Instead, it weaves into daily interactions, seemingly harmless comments, and supposedly "caring" gestures. When its presence is felt, it's often deeply entrenched, causing psychological scars that aren't easily visible.

The confidence you once held dear erodes, replaced by persistent self-doubt. Every compliment is viewed with suspicion, every criticism magnified. The world begins to feel like a maze where every turn is a potential trap. It's an endless cycle of trying not to upset the apple cart, of "walking on eggshells."

Paranoia, a word we never wish to associate with our personal lives, becomes an unwelcome guest. Trusting oneself becomes an uphill task. And as this web of manipulation wraps tighter, that voice – the one that once stood firm, asserting your wants, needs, and beliefs – starts to fade.

It might feel isolating, but remember, you're not alone. Understanding the onset of manipulation and acknowledging its presence is the beginning of reclaiming your voice, confidence, and, ultimately, life.

THE CONCEPT OF COGNITIVE DISSONANCE

I recall a session, years into my practice, with a woman named Tiffany. She painted a vivid picture of her partner's unpredictable behaviors. "He'd declare his undying love one day, and the next, he'd act cold and distant," she lamented. "But when I tried to discuss it, he'd insist everything was 'fine,' leaving me feeling like I was losing my grip on reality."

Tiffany's confusion was reminiscent of a psychological phenomenon I'd encountered countless times: cognitive dissonance. At its core, cognitive dissonance refers to the intense discomfort we feel when simultaneously holding two conflicting beliefs or values. It's akin to an emotional whirlwind, being pulled in different directions by our own mind.

Imagine you're a staunch vegetarian for ethical reasons, but one day, you unknowingly enjoy a meat dish. The internal conflict between your belief (eating meat is unethical) and your action (enjoying the dish) is cognitive dissonance.

Now, transfer this to the realm of toxic relationships. You believe your partner loves you based on their words. Yet, their actions suggest otherwise. This stark contradiction creates a turbulent internal conflict. "Do they genuinely love me, or am I misinterpreting their actions?" you might wonder.

Manipulators, sensing this internal rift, exploit it masterfully. They fuel the ambiguity, ensuring you're continuously doubting your perceptions. Over time, this self-doubt erodes your confidence, making it easier for them to maintain control. It's their twisted safety net.

Understanding cognitive dissonance is a lifeline. Recognizing it not only clears the haze but also reaffirms trust in oneself. You begin to see the patterns, trust your intuition, and challenge the manipulator's narrative. Your feelings, perceptions, and experiences are valid. Never let anyone, especially a manipulator, convince you otherwise.

DEFEATING YOUR MANIPULATOR

Let's dive into the nitty-gritty—how to take the reins back from a manipulative partner. I once worked with a client named Jonathon, who thought manipulation was just part of the "game of love." He would tell me, " I can't figure her out. One minute, she's sweet; the next, she's cold as ice. But isn't that what keeps the spark alive?"

Oh boy, did we have some unraveling to do. Jonathon soon realized that the "spark" he thought was romantic tension was actually a cycle of manipulation. The allure of unpredictability is a classic trick that manipulators use to keep you on your toes so you're never entirely grounded enough to see the bigger picture. It's not the spark, it's the trap.

Set Your Boundaries, and Stick to Them

Don't make your boundaries as flexible as a yoga instructor on a good day. Make them as solid as a brick wall. Manipulators often test your limits, gauging how far they can push you. If you give an inch, they'll take a mile. It's about regaining control. You have the right to say, "Enough!"

Keep a Record

You're not aiming for a bestselling memoir here, but jotting down incidents can be highly revealing. Document times when you felt manipulated, disrespected, or unheard. This isn't just for future reference but also to validate your feelings and experiences. Writing it down can be a self-affirming action that helps you see the manipulation for what it is.

Seek Support, But Choose Wisely

Manipulators often isolate their victims. Make a conscious effort to keep the lines of communication open with trusted friends and family. However, be cautious. Not everyone understands the nuances of manipulation. Stick with those who do, and consider speaking to a mental health professional. I've seen how validation can change the game.

Know When to Seek Professional Help

In extreme cases, you should involve a legal authority, especially if your physical safety is at risk. Don't let shame or fear stop you from taking this step. It's not a sign of weakness; it's a declaration of strength.

Future-Proof Your Love Life

When you're ready to move on, and you will be, remember that old habits die hard. It's easy to gloss over red flags in the honeymoon phase of future relationships. But you're wiser now. And the next time someone tries to tell you that "you're too sensitive" or "you're overthinking," you'll know better than to doubt yourself.

Let me be clear: none of this is a cakewalk. It's a process. Some days, it might feel like you're climbing a mountain with a boulder tied to your ankles. But every step you take is a move toward reclaiming your emotional freedom.

The desire for unconditional love is universal, and don't you ever feel guilty for wanting it. You deserve to be in a relationship where you are seen, heard, and valued, not one where you're constantly questioning your worth.

TRAPPED IN THE WEB

Thirty years in the counseling business, and there's a pattern that never ceases to amaze me. It's like a spider spinning its web, delicately and meticulously, around unsuspecting prey. The prey believes they are in a safe space, only to later find themselves stuck, with the net tightening around them. And trust me, this web isn't spun overnight.

Take Candace, for instance. She is a lively dance instructor, someone you'd imagine to be in control and on her feet, literally and metaphorically. Yet, she finds herself trapped by Phil's intricate web. The constant questioning, the need for location updates, GPS devices on her car—it's nothing short of espionage! The dance studio, her sanctuary, wasn't spared either. Her passion and escape became another place for Phil to invade and scrutinize. And Candace kept dancing, but on a web, not on a floor.

And then there's Abigail, a hardworking pharmacy technician, diligently filling prescriptions by day, only to go home and face a barrage of suspicions by night. Robert's web is woven with threads of mistrust and wild accusations. How does one even flirt while picking up broccoli and bell peppers for dinner? It sounds ridiculous, right? But for Abigail, it's her reality. The constant validation and presenting timesheets are exhausting.

I remember when I had a patient who said she couldn't even go to the neighborhood park because her partner would accuse her of going there to meet someone. It reminds me so much of these two ladies.

Now, you might be wondering, why don't they just leave? Well, the answer isn't straightforward. For many, there's a fear factor involved. For others, the manipulator might be their financial lifeline. And some simply believe, hope against hope, that things will change.

Candace and Abigail are being micromanaged, a manipulation tactic to exert control. These individuals want their partners to be answerable for every minute, every second. But here's the thing: it's not out of love; it's out of the need to control.

If you find hints of Candace's or Abigail's stories in your life, know this: no love story should feel like a detective thriller. Love trusts; it doesn't track.

If you justify your partner's actions, brushing them off as signs of 'care' or 'protection,' it might be time for introspection. And always remember, seeking professional help isn't a sign of weakness. It's a step towards reclaiming your narrative.

I've always believed in the power of introspection. The stories of Candace and Abigail might have stirred something inside you, or perhaps you saw a fragment of your own story in theirs. So, let's journey together into a self-reflective space. Grab a notepad, or just mentally note your responses. Ready?

1. When was the last time you felt the need to justify your actions or whereabouts to your

partner? Did it feel like a casual conversation or an interrogation?

2. Think about a week in your life. How often are you adjusting your routine, not for yourself, but to avoid confrontations or suspicions?

3. Recall a time when you felt truly free in your relationship, with no boundaries or fears. How does that memory make you feel in comparison to your current reality?

4. Have you refrained from attending events, meetings, or even casual gatherings because you anticipated adverse reactions from your partner? What was your rationale?

5. Can you pinpoint moments in your relationship when you felt like your personal space or privacy was invaded? How did you address it?

6. Think of a close friend or family member. Would you want them in a relationship that mirrors yours? Why or why not?

7. Do you often daydream or wish for a relationship where you feel more understood and valued?

8. Have you recently felt the urge to confide in someone about your relationship but held back due to fear of judgment or the implications it might have?

TOXIC RELATIONSHIPS | 91

9. On a scale of 1-10, how validated do you feel in your relationship? And how often do you feel the need to seek validation?

10. Lastly, what's one thing you wish you could change in your relationship? Why haven't you addressed it yet?

Years ago, I sat across from a woman, teary-eyed and broken, clutching a tissue as if it held her world together. She whispered, "I feel trapped, and the worst part is, the cage is invisible." It broke my heart. But her journey of self-realization began with self-reflection.

I hope these questions give you a clearer picture, not to judge, but to understand your feelings and where you stand. Sometimes, it's in understanding our current situation that we find the clarity and courage to make decisions for our future. Remember, this journey is yours, and I'm just here, sharing stories, wisdom, and a few nudges along the way.

I used to frequent an old amusement park just a few towns from where I practiced. The roller coaster there, nicknamed "The Emotional Tornado," was notorious for its thrilling highs and terrifying lows. People would queue for hours, anticipating the adrenaline rush, the joy, the fear, and the whole spectrum of emotions that came with it.

Sounds exhilarating, right? Now, imagine if that roller coaster never ended. Imagine if the exhilarating highs were short-lived, and the lows, stomach-churning and harrowing, persisted for longer than they should. That initial thrill of being on "The Emotional Tornado" would quickly turn into a wish to disembark, to find steady ground again. But what if you couldn't? What if the ride just kept going?

This is akin to being in a toxic relationship. Though often intoxicating, the highs can blind us to the impending lows. The manipulations and mind games are all there, twisting and turning your emotions, much like that roller coaster. But unlike "The Emotional Tornado," where you can choose to exit after the ride, the cycle of a toxic relationship isn't so easily broken. And the repercussions are far more profound.

It's no surprise that many find themselves stuck on this emotional ride. The highs, or the good times, act like a mirage, creating an illusion that everything will be alright, that maybe the next loop won't be as dizzying, or the next drop won't be as steep. But they are. Over and over again.

A few years back, a client confided in me about her relationship. She said, "I'm on this never-ending roller coaster. Whenever I think it's improving, I'm plunged back into darkness." The sadness in her eyes mirrored the countless others who felt trapped in this relentless ride.

But you know what? Like at the amusement park, every roller coaster has a control room. It's high time we explored the mechanics, understood the control panels, and learned how to bring this tumultuous ride to a halt. Not just for a break but to disembark, find our footing, and perhaps choose a different ride—one where the highs and lows balance each other out, where the journey is more joy than dread.

4

THE EMOTIONAL ROLLER COASTER RIDE

"Sometimes walking away has nothing to do with weakness and everything to do with strength. We walk away not because we want others to realize our worth and value, but because we finally realize our own."

— ANONYMOUS

In human relationships, some patterns emerge more vividly than others, weaving their way through our lives, pulling at the threads of our emotions, and sometimes tangling us in a web of confusion and pain. The intricacies of these patterns can be perplexing, and their effects overwhelming. I've witnessed countless tales of love, heartbreak, and dreams built and shattered. One pattern that emerges often and with profound impact is that of the emotional roller coaster that we discussed earlier – the highs of intense love, punctuated by the jolting lows of manipulation and control. Through this chapter, we'll embark on a journey to explore the underbelly of such toxic relationships. We'll dive deep into understanding the cycle that keeps many trapped in a dance of pain and love.

The Cycle of Toxicity

I remember sitting across from Marianne, a spirited woman in her early thirties. Tears welled in her eyes as she said, "Every time we fight, he brings me flowers the next day. The sweetness doesn't last, though. It's like a short-lived sunny day before another storm." As we delved deeper, we unraveled the repeating patterns of her relationship. Let's discuss this familiar dance that countless individuals like Marianne, find themselves trapped in: the cycle of toxicity.

1. Honeymoon Phase: Oh, the honeymoon phase! This period is often filled with love bombs. Everything feels perfect. Your partner showers you with affection and surprises and might even plan a future together. Remember the early days of Marianne's relationship? He'd bring her breakfast in bed and whisper sweet nothings.

TOXIC RELATIONSHIPS | 97

Imagine a relationship where, after every argument, there's a brief period where your partner becomes the ideal lover. They might write you love letters, or they'll suddenly be interested in the things you're passionate about. You think things have changed. But alas...

2. Tension Building: The skies gradually turn gray. Small annoyances grow. There's an unease in the air, like the tension before a storm. It's a period of walking on eggshells. Marianne mentioned how she'd avoid specific topics, fearful of igniting another argument.

Think of this as a pot of water on a stove. The heat rises, and tiny bubbles form. These are the minor irritations, the passive-aggressive comments, or the cold shoulder that can last for days.

3. Incident: The storm hits. The pot overflows. It's the explosion or breakdown where the actual abuse occurs – emotional, physical, or verbal. In Marianne's words, "It's as if a switch flips, and I no longer recognize him."

That ignored text or missed call turns into a full-blown argument. Accusations fly, hurtful words are exchanged, or worse, it escalates to physical confrontations.

4. Reconciliation: Once the storm subsides, there's an effort to mend the damage. There are apologies, promises, and tears. "I'll change," they'd swear.

Marianne's partner would cry, holding her close, vowing never to hurt her again.

It's like that movie scene where, after a huge fight, one partner shows up at the other's door, boombox in hand, playing their love song. It's romantic in movies, but in real life, it's often a sign of the cycle continuing.

5. Calm: A deceptive peace. The storm's aftermath. Things return to "normal." There's hope that things will be different this time. But without actual intervention and change, it's merely the calm before the next storm.

Days or weeks where everything seems fine. The house is peaceful, laughter returns, and you might share good times. But deep down, there's a nagging feeling, a whisper of the cycle possibly repeating itself.

If you recognize these patterns, know you're not alone. Marianne, like many, eventually saw the pattern and sought help. Understanding the cycle is the first step. Awareness can be a guiding light, leading you out of the storm and into sunnier days. Remember, you're worthy of a love that doesn't come with a storm warning.

UNDERSTANDING WHY YOU'RE TRAPPED

Have you ever found yourself riding a merry-go-round at a carnival? It's enchanting at first. The colorful lights, the captivating music, the sense of whimsical nostalgia. You hop onto one of those ornate horses, anticipating a fun ride. But after a few rounds, the charm fades. The repetitive circles make you dizzy, the music grates on your ears, and you're ready to get off. Yet, an unseen force holds you back as you reach out to disembark. The ride doesn't stop. The world outside the merry-go-round becomes a blur; the only reality is that relentless, never-ending cycle.

This is eerily similar to the dynamics of a toxic relationship. But why, despite the emotional dizziness and the loud clangs of alarm bells, do some find it seemingly impossible to step off that ride?

Psychologically speaking, people often find themselves trapped for several reasons. First and foremost is love. Many say, "But I love them." Yes, love is powerful. But it's essential to differentiate between love and dependency. Love should lift you, not weigh you down.

Then there's hope. "They'll change" is a common refrain. I've seen many, over the years, holding onto a glimmer of the person they first fell in love with. But waiting for someone to change can sometimes be like waiting for a train at an abandoned station.

External factors exert their force, too. Societal expectations can be suffocating. In many cultures, maintaining the facade of a 'happy relationship' or 'perfect marriage' is paramount, even if it's corroding one's soul from the inside. Familial pressures, especially when children are involved, add another layer of complexity. "What will people say?" is a haunting question for many.

Financial dependencies can't be ignored either. I remember when I had a client, Eliza. She was a brilliant woman, a university professor. But after marriage, her controlling partner convinced her to give up her job. With no personal income and two kids to think about, she felt like a bird with clipped wings.

The highs and lows of these relationships have an almost addictive quality. A toxic partner's manipulation might make you feel invaluable during the good times but worthless during the lows. This push-and-pull leaves many in constant emotional turmoil, seeking those fleeting moments of happiness and validation.

It's crucial, however, to remember that understanding why you're trapped is the first step towards finding the exit. Once you pinpoint the chains binding you, you can work on breaking them, one link at a time.

In the end, remember that you deserve a ride that's exhilarating and joyful, not one that leaves you yearning to escape. The world outside the merry-go-round is vast and full of opportunities. It's time to explore it.

BREAKING THE CHAINS ISN'T EASY

I had a session with a woman named Leila. Her story was one of strength, resilience, and immense courage. She was in the process of leaving a relationship that had drained her emotionally for nearly a decade. As she sat across from me, I remember the weight of her emotions filling the room—all interwoven- grief, hope, fear, and determination.

"Every time I packed my bags," she whispered, her voice trembling, "a voice inside me would say, 'Maybe today was just a bad day. Tomorrow will be better.' And like a broken record, I'd unpack, hoping for that elusive 'better tomorrow.'"

Many, like Leila, grapple with deep-rooted emotional barriers. Guilt is a heavy chain. They question if they've done enough, tried hard enough, or are abandoning someone they once promised to stand by. Then there's shame. It's as if admitting the toxicity means admitting their failure to make it work.

Fear of retaliation is another enormous barrier. For some, this fear is physical, fearing violence or harm. For others, it's more subtle—a haunting apprehension about emotional or financial revenge.

The mental challenges are intricately layered. Cognitive dissonance is a term we therapists use a lot. As mentioned previously, It's the mental discomfort one feels when their actions don't align with their beliefs. In toxic relationships, it manifests as "He loves me, so why does he hurt me?" or "She says she cares, but her actions show otherwise." This dissonance forces many to change their actions (like leaving) or adjust their beliefs to reduce the discomfort. Sadly, many end up convincing themselves that they deserve the treatment they're getting.

Self-blame and low self-esteem feed off each other in a vicious cycle. The toxic partner might constantly belittle or criticize, which erodes self-worth. And as self-worth diminishes, the victim often blames themselves more, thinking, "Maybe if I were better/smarter/more attractive, things would be different."

Practical complexities add another dimension. Leila, for instance, shared bank accounts and property with her partner. Shared finances become tangled webs that are challenging to untwine. And for those with children, co-parenting introduces an array of challenges.

How do you protect your children while freeing yourself?

Lastly, stepping out can sometimes feel like stepping into an abyss of judgment. The potential for societal backlash is real. Close friends or family might advise reconciliation, often without understanding the depth of the pain. Some might face isolation, either by choice or as a consequence of societal shunning.

Leaving isn't a mere physical act of walking away. It's an intricate dance of navigating emotional, mental, and practical landmines. But as Leila told me months later, "Every step away from him felt like a step closer to myself." Remember that. With every struggle and challenge faced head-on, you're journeying towards a life where you can once again breathe freely, laugh wholeheartedly, and live authentically.

A LOOK AT ATTACHMENT STYLES

In my early days as a therapist, I had a patient named Linda. She was an eloquent, kind-hearted woman with sparkling eyes. Yet, behind those eyes, I saw a torrent of emotions, often dominated by anxiety and fear. We embarked on a journey to delve into the core of her feelings, eventually leading us to discuss attachment theory.

Attachment theory, rooted deeply in our developmental stages, suggests that our early relationships with our primary caregivers, mainly our parents, pave the path for how we perceive and act in relationships later in life. It is as if our past casts shadows, influencing our present connections and interactions.

Most people I've worked with aren't aware of the distinct attachment styles, yet they resonate deeply once revealed:

1. **Secure Attachment**: Imagine being in a relationship where you're comfortable being close and don't fear being alone. It's like sitting in your favorite armchair with a warm blanket wrapped around you. For instance, I chatted with a young woman named Ella. She said: "Even when we argue, we will sort it out. He's my anchor."

2. **Anxious Attachment**: Do you ever feel like you're constantly seeking reassurance? Fearful that you're not loved or worried about being too much or needy? That's the anxious attachment style. Remember Linda? She once said, "Every time he's late, my mind convinces me he's either met someone else or is lying somewhere in a ditch."

3. **Avoidant Attachment**: Picture someone fiercely protective of their independence, often pushing others away, fearing intimacy. It's like they have an invisible shield. David, a man in his forties I once counseled, exemplified this, saying, "I like my space. When things get too intense, I need to step back."

4. **Anxious-Avoidant Attachment**: This one's a cocktail of anxiety and avoidance. Individuals with this style are in a constant dilemma – craving intimacy but deeply fearing it. "It's like wanting to jump into the water but being terrified of the deep end," a gentleman named Mark once told me.

What's intriguing is that many with anxious attachment styles are magnetized to toxic relationships. It's not a conscious choice but a yearning to fill an emotional void, a hope that 'this person' might fill the gaps left from childhood. But sadly, they often end up with partners who confirm their worst fears, leading them to believe they aren't worth loving.

But here's the silver lining: Attachment styles aren't set in stone. Our brains are incredible, adaptive organs. With awareness, patience, therapy, and sometimes even with the support of a trustworthy partner, you can journey from insecure attachment styles to a secure one.

For those with anxious attachment:

1. **Recognize your pattern**: The first step is acknowledgment. Are you continually seeking validation? Understand that this is a learned behavior and not a character flaw.
2. **Communicate**: Share your feelings with your partner. Remember, it's okay to be vulnerable. In the words of Dr. Brené Brown, "Vulnerability is the birthplace of love, belonging, and joy."
3. **Self-soothe**: Develop techniques to comfort yourself in times of anxiety. It could be meditation, journaling, or simply taking a walk.
4. **Therapy**: Sometimes, diving into your past with a professional can open doors to understanding and healing.

Remember, you're not chained to your past. You have the power to redefine your future. Embrace your attachment style, understand it, and take steps to reshape it if needed. It's a journey to your heart, and trust me, it's worth every step.

WHISPERS AND SHOUTS: MELINDA AND GINGER'S STORIES

Around three decades ago, during one of my early counseling sessions, a distressed young woman asked me, "Why does love have to be so painfully complex?" It's a question I've often encountered in different forms in my years of practice. The intricate web of emotions in relationships, especially toxic ones, has baffled many. Enter Melinda and Ginger.

Melinda, 57, has been on a roller coaster ride for over 20 years with Bill. From my vantage, it's been a dizzying mix of soaring highs and harrowing plunges. Bill's consistent emotional and verbal abuse was peppered with periodic "love bombs." Remember the term 'love bombing'? It's a manipulative tactic where the abuser showers their partner with excessive affection and attention, only to use it as leverage later. Melinda would often sit across from me, teary-eyed, and say, "How could I be so terrible and wonderful at the same time?" The confusion she felt is characteristic of many in her shoes. It's like trying to decipher a distorted reflection. You know it's you, but the image keeps changing. The truth is, she's neither terrible nor the most wonderful woman in the world. She's human, deserving of consistent love and respect.

Now, Ginger's story hits differently. Married to Jay for 12 years, her life reads like a slow-burning suspense thriller. His manipulative prowess darkly shadows Jay's abuse. He's isolated her so much from family and friends that she often laments about the bridges she feels she's burnt. Here's the paradox: Ginger wants out, but the chains of fear have a vice-like grip on her. She often shared, "I wonder if they'll be there for me. And what if Jay does something to himself or, worse, to me?" Staying, in her mind, seems the lesser of two evils.

Relating these stories to our earlier discourse on attachment styles, both women show traces of anxious attachment. The constant need for validation, the insatiable desire to be loved, and the fear of abandonment anchor them to these toxic relationships. Their stories aren't uncommon. Trust me; I've seen many Melindas and Gingers in my practice.

But if there's one thing I'd like you to take away from these narratives, it's this: understanding is the first step to healing. Recognizing the signs, the patterns, and the internal dialogues can empower individuals to seek change. Both Melinda and Ginger, despite their situations, show remarkable strength. It's just misdirected. The journey might be long and challenging, but the destination is worth it. Safe, healthy love is not a myth;

it's attainable. And while the path may seem daunting, remember, every journey begins with a single step.

Toward the end of one session, I remember telling Melinda, "Love isn't supposed to be a puzzle. It's meant to be a picture." And to you, let's work together on piecing that picture together.

It's one thing to read about Melinda and Ginger, but it's another to reflect on our own experiences and perhaps spot those shadows of similarity in our lives. By sharing their stories, I invite you to embark on a journey of introspection. Are you seated comfortably? Alright, then, let's dive in.

1. Emotional Whiplash: Remember how Melinda was constantly tossed between being 'terrible' and 'wonderful'? Have you ever felt like you're riding the highs and lows of someone else's opinion of you?

Take a moment. Jot down instances where you felt like you were on top of the world, only to be brought crashing down soon after.

2. Connections and Isolations: Ginger's tale is a grim reminder of how easy it is to lose oneself in the maze of manipulation. Do you feel like there are people, hobbies, or passions you've drifted away from due to your relationship?

Maybe it's that friend you used to laugh with or that dance class you once loved. Write them down.

3. The Financial Tug: A stable job doesn't always equate to financial independence, especially when one's partner holds the purse strings. Do you feel like you're in complete control of your financial decisions?

Pause and think of the last big purchase you wanted to make. Did you consult someone? Were you afraid of their reaction?

4. The Silent Pleas: We all want to make someone proud – our family, friends, or society. But at what cost? Who are you trying to please in your relationship? And, more importantly, why?

List down those names or societal norms. Next to each, write what you believe they expect from you.

5. The Innermost Craving: Here's a toughie. We all yearn for love, respect, and understanding. In your quietest moments, what does your heart whisper?

Don't rush this. It might be a simple phrase or a vivid memory. Capture that.

6. The Advice Trap: "Just leave." We've all heard it, haven't we? What advice have you received that felt oversimplified or ignorant of your intricate circumstances?

Recall those conversations. How did they make you feel? What would you have wanted to hear instead?

A client handed me a wrinkled piece of paper filled with her answers. Tear stains smudged her words, but the clarity in her eyes was unmistakable. She told me, "This exercise is like turning on a light in a room I didn't know existed within me." And you know, I believe it can do the same for you.

So, take your time with this. This isn't a race, nor is it a test. It's a small pit-stop in our journey together, a chance to refuel and reorient before we move forward.

As a psychotherapist, I've had countless clients walk into my office, hoping for the magic wand that'll make the pain from toxic relationships vanish. Many believe that they've crossed the finish line once they identify the toxicity and decide to break free. But here's the harsh truth: that's just the starting pistol firing. You've done something phenomenal, but the race, my dear, has just begun.

A decade ago, I had a client, Eleanor. She was a fire-cracker - full of spirit, wit, and a penchant for painting her nails bright orange. Eleanor told me, "Walking away was like ripping off a Band-Aid. Quick, painful, but done. Now, I'm staring at the wound and don't know what to do with it." That profound analogy resonated deeply with me.

When we muster the courage to sever ties with toxicity, we're often left with this gaping wound, these uncharted waters of rediscovery, healing, and self-compassion. The questions linger: "What next? How do I heal? How do I ensure I don't find myself in the same predicament?"

I've watched many sunsets from my office window, reflecting on these questions and how best to guide those in turmoil. To those who've taken the brave step, kudos! It's a testament to your strength. But just as a sailor doesn't stop sailing after surviving a storm, you, too, shouldn't stop navigating your emotional seas after escaping a toxic relationship.

You may wonder why we're spending time diving deep into the manipulations and emotional roller-coasters of such relationships. Well, it's because understanding is the first step to healing. When we can identify and name the monsters that haunt us, they lose some power over us.

We will delve into the essential journey of healing in the chapters to come. How do you rebuild trust, not just in others, but in yourself? How do you reclaim your identity? How do you ensure history doesn't repeat itself?

So, as we turn the page, let's remember: life doesn't give us a GPS, especially not for the treacherous terrains of our emotions. But together, we can find our way. Remember that there's a guiding star within you through the storms, the calm, and the in-betweens.

5

SHADOWS OF THE FORMER SELF

"Sometimes the hardest part isn't letting go, but rather realizing that you have changed."

— LEONARD JACOBSON

Years ago, I had a client, John, a passionate chef who had once been known for his culinary brilliance. When he walked into my office, it was evident that the spark in his eyes had faded, and the vibrant flavors he once created in the kitchen were now lost in a cloud of turmoil from his relationship. John's story is all too relatable for many of you. That vibrant, passionate person you used to be can become overshadowed by a version of yourself molded by someone else's desires.

We all have an innate essence, a core identity that shines through when we're most genuine. Yet, toxic relationships have an uncanny way of casting a shadow over that light, slowly but surely. It's like trying to recognize your face in a tarnished mirror. You know it's you, but the reflection staring back seems distant, distorted, and unfamiliar.

In this chapter, we will navigate the winding paths of self-alteration, probing into how a toxic relationship can shift the very core of who we are. Through anecdotes and insights, we will recognize the signs, understand the psychological factors, and, most importantly, discuss ways to reclaim our lost selves.

HOW TOXIC LOVE ERODES SELF-IMAGE

Think back to a time when you admired yourself in a pristine mirror. The reflection staring back at you was clear, unblemished, and authentic. That mirror symbolizes your self-image before the storm of a toxic relationship. Now, imagine that same mirror with an intricate web of cracks running through it. It's harder to see your true self, isn't it? You might even start believing the distorted reflection is the real you. And that's precisely what happens when toxicity seeps into our lives.

I remember counseling a gentleman in his late thirties. He was a teacher known for his infectious laughter and undying enthusiasm. But two years into a toxic relationship, he confessed, "I barely recognize the man in the mirror. It's as if he's taken my spirit away." This profound erosion of self-worth isn't overnight; it's a gradual process. Like that mirror collecting dust and cracks over time, one hardly notices the change until it's overwhelming.

So, how does a toxic relationship chip away at our self-esteem? Let's delve deep:

1. **Constant Criticism**: Every relationship has its disagreements. But in a toxic relationship, these disagreements morph into continuous criticism, targeting one's core self rather than just the behavior. It's no longer about what you did but who you are.

2. **Comparisons with Others**: "Why can't you be more like her?" Sound familiar? Being unfavorably compared to others, especially consistently, can make one feel never good enough.

3. **Invalidation of Feelings**: Have you ever heard, "You're overreacting" or "You're too sensitive?" Continual invalidation can lead someone to distrust their feelings, judgment, and intuition.

4. **Isolation from Support Systems**: A classic sign. The toxic partner often chips away at one's self-worth by cutting them off from friends and family, those who usually remind them of their worth.

5. **Gaslighting**: This term comes up often, but few truly grasp its depth. Gaslighting makes someone question their reality, making them dependent on their partner for "truth."

Years ago, a bright-eyed woman, Grace, stepped into my office. She had given up painting, her life's passion, because her partner felt it was "a childish pursuit." It took months for her to realize she had sacrificed a part of herself, all because her self-worth was tethered to his perceptions.

Toxic relationships are akin to being trapped in quicksand. The more you struggle without awareness, the deeper you sink. But acknowledging and understanding these erosions is the first step in pulling yourself out. And trust me, with the right tools and support, it's possible to cleanse that marred mirror and rediscover the incredible person staring back. Remember, the cracks in the mirror aren't in you; they're external. Your core remains untouched, waiting to shine once more.

Throughout my years of counseling, one recurring story has been individuals feeling like shadows of their former selves. It's as though they're living in a dense fog, unable to recall who they were before the relationship began. It's a heart-wrenching realization when someone tells me, "I don't recognize the person in the mirror anymore." So, let's delve into the chilling phenomenon of losing oneself to a relationship's overpowering demands.

Several years ago, a bright, vivacious artist named Chloe came into my office. She was the life of every gathering, brimming with tales of her artistic pursuits. But after a particularly demanding relationship, her spark seemed dimmed. Chloe, like many, had lost significant parts of herself to meet her partner's needs. She gave up painting, stopped seeing her closest friends, and slowly, her once-lived world shrank.

Now, let me get a bit technical, but bear with me. Self-image is our mental representation of ourselves. It's how we see our traits, beliefs, and role in the world. A healthy self-image contributes to overall well-being, whereas a poor one can lead to anxiety, depression, and stagnation. In a toxic relationship, an individual's self-image often gets entangled with their partner's perception, leading them to sideline their needs, wants, and aspirations.

You see, toxic love doesn't just show up one day, demanding you change. It's far more insidious. It starts as a whisper, suggesting you skip that evening class to spend more time together. It's the gentle nudge that you should dress more modestly or the off-hand remark about how you've changed since you started that new job—each concession, each change, chips away at the self-image until there's hardly any self left.

I've noticed a pattern in such relationships:

1. **Silencing oneself**: Holding back on opinions or decisions to avoid conflicts.
2. **Isolation**: Slowly cutting ties with friends and family, thereby losing important feedback loops that remind you of who you are.
3. **Abandoning personal passions**: Painting, music, or any hobby that once gave joy.
4. **Adopting the partner's identity**: Their likes and dislikes, opinions, and life goals.
5. **Decreased self-worth**: Relying heavily on the partner for validation and acceptance.

A crucial aspect of our well-being is our self-image. It dictates how we interact with the world, our choices, and how we feel about ourselves. In the cruel hands of a toxic relationship, this self-image gets distorted. Every cruel word, every time we're made to feel not good enough, takes a toll. When our self-worth is measured through someone else's ever-shifting lens, the reflection can be painful.

But here's the part I want you to hold on to — even if the mirror of your self-worth feels cracked, remember that mirrors can be mended. You've taken the brave step of acknowledging the distortion. You can rebuild a strong, healthy self-image with understanding, self-love, and professional guidance. Don't let anyone, no matter how intimate, hold the power to define your worth. It's time to reclaim the narrative of your life.

IMPROVING YOUR SELF-IMAGE

In my many years of counseling, I've seen countless resilient individuals who, despite the odds, find the strength to rise. In the quiet rooms of my practice, I've held space for teary eyes, broken hearts, and yet, amidst it all, an undying spirit. Believe me when I say though your self-image may feel like a faded, tattered photo-graph right now, it can be restored, vibrant, and full of life once more.

I remember when I sat down with a 34-year-old woman named Anna. Her story still lingers with me. She said, "I used to be someone who'd light up a room, but now I barely recognize myself in the mirror." Anna's story, and perhaps yours too, isn't just about heartbreak; it's about rediscovery. So, let's embark on this journey together.

REDISCOVERING YOUR WORTH

1. **Embrace Self-Affirmations:** I often advise my clients to talk to themselves as they would to a dear friend. Simple affirmations like "I deserve love" or "I trust my intuition" work wonders. When Anna began challenging the negative self-talk with positive affirmations, she began to see herself differently.

2. **Pursue Your Passions:** Remember when you spent hours painting, dancing, or writing? When was the last time you did that? Engaging in activities that once brought joy can reignite a lost spark. Find that old guitar, put on your dancing shoes, and watch how the world changes.

3. **Seeking Therapy:** Oh, I've shared a number of "Aha!" moments with clients! Sometimes, having a professional help you untangle the

web of thoughts can be a game-changer. There's no shame in seeking help. You wouldn't hesitate to see a doctor for a broken arm, would you?

4. **Surround Yourself with Positive Influences:** Toxicity can become our norm, but once we step out, we see a world filled with love and positivity. Start by surrounding yourself with those who lift you up. They're the ones who'll be your safety net, your cheerleaders.

THE JOURNEY OF SELF-RECONSTRUCTION

Now, this is a process that takes time. Think of it as restoring an old painting. It takes time, patience, and sometimes, repeatedly going back over the same spots. But oh, the result is worth it!

Celebrate the small victories. Maybe it's the day you looked in the mirror and smiled genuinely. Or it's when you stand up for yourself in a conversation. Every step counts.

And here's your call to action: Start today. Right now. Maybe with a simple affirmation, by reaching out to a therapist, or even dancing in your living room like no one's watching. Your journey to rebuild begins with a single step.

And if Anna's story resonates, know that today she's rediscovered her joy, and while her journey continues, she's again painting her world with vibrant colors. And believe me, you can too. Remember, every story has its chapters, and this chapter about rediscovering your self-image will be one for the books.

THE PSYCHOLOGY OF ENDURING PAIN

In my three decades of counseling, I've witnessed countless stories of individuals losing themselves in toxic relationships. The intricacies of these narratives are as unique as the people living them. Yet, a common thread weaves through each one: suppressed emotions and the mechanisms we use to endure pain.

I met Tamara, a 45-year-old accomplished manager at a renowned software firm, years ago. She came to me with complaints of persistent insomnia and an increasing sense of desolation. Over our sessions, the source of her distress emerged. Her husband's constant belittling had subtly compelled her to suppress her feelings to the point where she couldn't even recognize her own emotional state. Whenever she'd hint at her unhappiness, he'd mock her, calling her "dramatic" or "too emotional." Like many, Tamara had, over time, started to believe it.

Suppressing our feelings might seem like a short-term solution. "If I don't acknowledge it, it'll go away," we might think. But our bodies are astute communicators. When we stifle our emotions, they manifest in other ways: tension headaches, that weight on our chest, or a sudden bout of inexplicable tears. Stress can present itself in more sinister forms, too. Chronic ailments like hypertension, digestive issues, and even heart diseases can be exacerbated by untreated emotional distress. For Tamara, her insomnia was just her body's way of nudging her, a desperate cry for attention.

Our mind, ingenious as it is, develops various strategies to help us cope with this prolonged emotional strain. Psychological defense mechanisms, like old friends trying to console us, come into play.

Denial was Tamara's defense. Whenever her colleagues commented on her husband's public displays of disdain, she'd shrug it off, saying they had a 'unique' sense of humor. Denial is a safety blanket, allowing us to dodge reality for a while. However, it's like putting a band-aid on a wound that needs stitches over time.

Projection, another defense mechanism, had also found its way into Lisa's relationship. She'd accuse colleagues of being 'condescending' or 'dismissive' even when they weren't. It was easier to pin those feelings on others than to accept that they stemmed from her marriage.

And then there's avoidance, which many of us are champions of. We keep busy and drown ourselves in work or hobbies—anything to sidestep the hurt. Tamara would bury herself in office tasks, volunteering for assignments she didn't need to. Overtime was her escape.

But here's what's crucial to understand: these defenses might feel like they're helping, but they're just stop-gap arrangements. They're those pesky notifications on our phones that we swipe away, but they keep popping back. Until one day, the phone crashed because we didn't address the underlying issue.

Why am I sharing Tamara's story? Not because it's unique but because it's not. Behind her story could be your face, your neighbor's, or even your best friend's. Our experiences might differ in detail, but the essence remains. We must recognize these suppressed emotions and defense mechanisms for what they are: signals.

The good news is that realization is half the battle won. Understanding our mind's strategies and our body's cues makes us better equipped to confront and heal. Remember, you deserve a relationship where you can voice your feelings without hesitation or fear of ridicule. It's never too late to reclaim yourself.

LOST IN THE MAZE: YOLANDA AND SUSAN'S STORIES

Years back, I was introduced to a brilliant engineer named Yolanda. Our conversations usually revolved around blueprints and mathematical models, but one day, the topic took a different turn. Yolanda shared her relationship struggles with her partner, James. James had an uncanny ability to make her feel like she was always in the wrong. If he said something hurtful, he would twist the situation, making it seem like Yolanda was the cause of his outburst. It's a classic "You made me do it" scenario. The constant blame game had Yolanda replaying events and conversations in her head, wondering if she was at fault. I could see the exhaustion in her eyes, the erosion of her self-worth, and the constant second-guessing of her judgment.

Similarly, I came to know Susan, a compassionate veterinarian. Susan had this infectious zeal for life, always talking about the animals she treated. However, when the topic of her partner Rebecca came up, her vivacity dimmed. Rebecca had mastered the silent treatment. She'd shut down if upset, leaving Susan emotionally stranded, sometimes for a week. And then, without warning, she'd return, acting like the silence had never happened. Susan was trapped in a maze of confusion, struggling to process her bottled-up emotions and wondering if she should be grateful that Rebecca was speaking to her again.

These stories might sound familiar to many of you. And let me tell you, it's a heartbreaking pattern I've witnessed countless times in my practice. The common thread? The distortion of self-worth and identity.

Yolanda's story is a classic example of gaslighting – a manipulative tactic where one person makes another question their reality. It's like being stuck in quicksand; the more you struggle, the deeper you sink. Deep down, Yolanda knew she wasn't to blame, but James' constant deflection made her second-guess her intuition.

Susan's situation is equally distressing. The silent treatment is a form of emotional abuse. By refusing to communicate, Rebecca exerted control over Susan, making her feel isolated and desperate for any form of acknowledgment. It's like being in a maze with no exit in sight.

Relating these stories to the broader picture, toxic relationships often have a pattern. They drain your self-esteem, make you question your worth, and trap you in a cycle of self-doubt. The tactics might vary, but the result is the same – a shadow of your former self.

For those of you reading this and seeing echoes of your own life in Yolanda or Susan's stories, please know you're not alone. Recognizing these patterns is a significant first step. Remember, it's not your fault. No one has the right to play with your emotions or make you feel less than.

As we journey further into this chapter, I hope to shed light on how to regain your sense of self. And maybe, just maybe, find the exit from that maze. Remember, you are not just a shadow; you are the light. And that light deserves to shine brilliantly.

The memory of Yolanda and Susan's experiences tugs at my heart even today. I've found that while every individual's situation is unique, specific emotional experiences are universal. You might find bits and pieces of your own life in their tales, or you may recognize someone you know.

So, let's pause for a moment and reflect. Let's dive deep and genuinely ask ourselves some tough, revealing questions. As I pose these questions, I encourage you to listen to that small voice inside you. The one often drowned out by life's chaos, the one that holds your truths.

1. Have you ever felt like your reality was being twisted by someone else? Like Yolanda, do you find yourself replaying events and questioning if you were really in the wrong?

2. In moments of introspection, have you identified patterns where you're being held emotionally hostage? Like Susan, do you feel stuck in a loop of silence, followed by a sudden return to normalcy, with no acknowledgment of the pain caused?

3. Are there instances where you've felt the need to suppress your emotions, to bury them deep down because you fear judgment or further isolation?

4. Remember when you truly felt free, unburdened, and completely yourself. How does that memory compare to your present reality? Is there a vast difference between who you were and who you are now?

5. When was the last time you felt truly seen, heard, and valued in your relationship?

6. Are there moments when you felt your self-worth erode because of the actions or words of someone close?

A couple of years ago, I met a young woman who had an epiphany while reflecting on these questions. She realized that while her relationship wasn't as overtly damaging as some, there were subtle undercurrents of toxicity that she had normalized. It was a slow erosion of self-worth, almost invisible but ever-present. She joked that it was like death by a thousand paper cuts, and I couldn't help but think how apt the comparison was.

Taking a moment to introspect isn't about self-blame; it's about self-awareness. It's about recognizing patterns, understanding our feelings, and reclaiming our sense of self.

Remember that this isn't about pointing fingers or assigning blame. This is your journey of self-discovery. Understanding our shadows gives us the strength to step into the light. Your past does not define your future; each day allows you to rewrite your story.

Embrace it with an open heart.

Chapter 5 has been quite a journey, hasn't it? We delved deep into the emotional intricacies of toxic relationships through Yolanda and Susan's stories. Each of their experiences painted a vivid picture of how these bonds can morph one's self-image and suffocate the very essence of who they are. My heart aches when I think of how many of you might've seen yourself or someone you love in their narratives.

As we close this chapter, I want to reflect on a personal encounter from my early years of counseling. I met a woman who had been in a toxic relationship for decades. One day, as she looked in the mirror, she realized she barely recognized the person staring back. This wasn't about age or physical appearance but about the absence of that spark in her eyes—the spark that once shone brightly, reflecting her dreams and ambitions. She whispered, "I feel like a shadow of my former self." It was heartbreaking but also enlightening. Her acknowledgment of that feeling was the first step towards breaking free.

I've seen countless individuals transform over the years, emerging stronger and more resilient after freeing themselves from toxic relationships. It isn't a linear process. There will be days filled with doubt and moments of vulnerability. But remember, even the most potent toxin loses its power once identified and understood.

So, where do we go from here? The shadows might seem overwhelming, but there's always a way out, even if it's not immediately evident. The next chapter promises a journey towards that light. It's about understanding, healing, and eventually rediscovering the extraordinary individual buried beneath those shadows.

6

BREAKING FREE

"When we face our fears, we can find our freedom."

— JOYCE MEYER

I 've crossed paths with many people who've felt imprisoned by the shackles of their toxic relation-ships. The irony is sometimes, these chains are more mental than physical. Remember, toxicity doesn't always announce its arrival with blaring sirens. It often tiptoes into our lives, establishing itself quietly and gradually. When we notice it, we might feel it's too late. But let me tell you, there is always time to seek freedom and well-being.

Think about it—haven't we all, at some point, ignored the little voice inside us that tries to alert us about something off in our relationships? Often, societal expectations, fear of loneliness, or financial constraints play a crucial role in silencing that voice.

Let me share a little story. About a decade ago, I encountered a man in his mid-40s. He was a high school teacher, passionate about his job, and loved by his students. But at home, he faced a completely different world. His wife, struggling with her issues, constantly belittled him. He said, "Thirty years ago, I wanted to be a novelist. My dream was silenced because she said it was impractical and childish." The sorrow in his eyes spoke volumes. But guess what? Today, he's published two novels and conducts creative writing workshops for young adults. He found his path to break free.

This chapter is about finding that path for yourself. Recognizing the toxicity is the first step, but what follows next? How do you navigate the maze of emotions, societal expectations, and practical constraints? I'll guide you through it, drawing from the experiences of numerous individuals I've had the privilege to help over the years. We'll delve deep into strategies, motivation, and the spark of hope that'll light your way forward because freedom is a beautiful thing. And you deserve every bit of it.

REALIZING THE NEED TO BREAK FREE

Ah, the moment of epiphany. That instant when the clouds part, you see your relationship for what it truly is: toxic. It might come to you like a lightning bolt during a heated argument or as a slow-dawning realization while sipping your morning coffee. It's as if a veil has been lifted, revealing a bitter truth you've been trying not to face. I remember sitting across from a client, Emma when she had her "aha" moment. "I feel like I'm drowning," she said. "And he's not throwing me a lifeline; he's handing me an anvil."

This realization is often accompanied by a cocktail of emotions: fear, guilt, uncertainty, but also—yes—a glimmer of hope and a dash of determination. You feel fear because you're venturing into the unknown. Guilt makes a guest appearance, too, whispering in your ear about commitments, promises, and perceived failures. But please don't forget that your newfound hope and determination are alongside these uneasy emotions. You start thinking, "Maybe, just maybe, I don't have to live like this."

So, what usually nudges you toward this vital awakening? It varies, but it could be a concerned friend who finally gets through to you, showing you that love doesn't mean perpetual misery. Or maybe you stumbled upon an article about emotional abuse and found it eerily relatable. Sometimes, it takes an extreme incident to serve as your wake-up call, like a scandalous betrayal or a particularly nasty argument that crosses several lines.

Before we dive into strategies, let's underline something crucial: trust your gut. Often, your intuition has been throwing warning signs at you like a street vendor tossing free samples. If you feel something's off, it probably is. Sometimes, the signs of toxicity aren't grand gestures of awfulness; they're subtle, creeping into your life like an unpleasant melody you can't shake. So, if your intuition is nudging you, give it the floor. Listen.

I know it's easier said than done, especially if you have been doubting your feelings and experiences due to the manipulative nature of toxic relationships. So, the first step is often reclaiming trust in your insights and judgments. You're not overreacting, you're not too sensitive, and you're not "crazy." You're waking up. And sometimes, waking up is uncomfortable; it's disorienting, but most importantly, necessary. You're on the brink of reclaiming your life, and trust me, the view from the other side? Absolutely stunning.

HOW TO DISTANCE ONESELF FROM A TOXIC PARTNER

Pulling back from someone you've given so much of yourself to is undeniably challenging. It's like untying a tight knot that's held together for years; you know it's necessary, where do you start?

Step one: **Set Clear Boundaries.** Let's be honest: boundary setting can be as awkward as running into an ex at the supermarket. But it's crucial. Be clear about what you're comfortable with, how often you'll communicate, or what topics are off-limits. A few years ago, a client set up "phone-free evenings." It gave her the space she needed without creating an outright war.

Step two: **Limit Shared Responsibilities.** Remember those couple's yoga classes? Or that joint bank account? It may be time to reassess. While not all shared responsibilities can be avoided, especially if children are involved, try to minimize where you can. You want to start building a life that's *yours*.

Step three: **Seek Professional Guidance.** Think of it as using a GPS while navigating unfamiliar territory. Sometimes, you need an unbiased guide to offer you a clear path. A therapist, counselor, or trustworthy mentor can provide invaluable insights.

Space, The Underrated Healer. There's a reason why people go on solo trips or retreats after a breakup. Space – both emotional and physical – can be incredibly therapeutic. I once knew a couple who decided to take a "relationship sabbatical." They lived apart for six months. While they didn't end up together, they both emerged with a better understanding of themselves and what they wanted.

And remember, distancing yourself doesn't mean you're giving up or admitting defeat. In many cases, it's a self-preservation technique. It's giving you room to breathe, think, and heal.

If I could turn back the clock and chat with my younger self, I'd say: You can't sip from an empty cup. You need to refill, recharge, and sometimes, recalibrate." This distancing? It's your way of ensuring that the next time you pour out love, understanding, or commitment, you're giving the best version of it. Because, after all, you deserve nothing less.

In the labyrinth of life, we often forget that not every turn is meant to be ventured alone. In distancing ourselves from a toxic partner, leaning on others can feel like a life raft, a beacon of hope in an otherwise stormy sea.

THE PILLARS OF SUPPORT

Back in the '90s, I had a friend named Denise. She was fiery, full of spirit, and fiercely independent. She often said, "I've got this," even when "this" was a relationship spiraling downwards. One day, she admitted, "I need help." It wasn't a sign of weakness but a moment of strength. That day, we listed out the people and places she could turn to.

1. **Friends and Family:** These are your frontline warriors. Even if you've grown apart or if they've been on the sidelines, reconnect. They've often seen the signs before you did and are waiting to support you. You'd be surprised how a simple heart-to-heart can lift the weight off your shoulders.

2. **Support Groups:** There's a unique strength in shared experiences. Groups, whether online or offline, bring together people who've walked the path, felt the pain, and have stories of resilience. Sometimes, knowing you're not alone in the journey is half the battle won.

3. **Therapy:** It is a space for guided introspection. I've witnessed countless individuals find their direction, armed with new coping mechanisms and the reassurance of an empathetic ear.

THE 'YOU' PRIORITY

Your well-being isn't a luxury; it's a necessity. And sometimes, prioritizing yourself requires making hard choices. I counseled a young man caught in a toxic whirlwind. He quipped, "I feel like I'm choosing between love and sanity." I replied, "Your love for yourself should always come first."

Here's the truth - we are conditioned to think of sacrifice as noble. But there's a difference between compromise and losing yourself. Remember, it's time to reassess if a relationship starts jeopardizing your peace, self-worth, or health

. This isn't me pushing you towards a decision. This is me nudging you to prioritize, to value your feelings, and to recognize when it's time to draw a line.

To sum it up, distancing from a toxic partner isn't just a solo act. It's a concert, a symphony of support from friends, family, professionals, and most importantly, your inner self. The harmony might seem off now, but with each passing note, the melody of freedom gets clearer.

Years from now, when you are reminiscing about your tough choices, you can celebrate the incredible journey it took to find yourself again. After all, every song has its highs and lows, but we remember the crescendo of triumph most.

SAFEGUARDING AGAINST POTENTIAL BACKLASH

It's been a privilege to accompany many courageous people on their journey to breaking free. As a therapist, I've seen that breaking away is just one part of the puzzle. The other part? Preparing for the aftermath.

Years ago, a client named Alexis opened up about her turbulent relationship. She used an analogy that still sticks with me today: "It's like trying to walk away from a storm while still getting drenched by the rain." Sometimes, leaving can stir up a storm from the other end – the toxic partner. Their reactions can range from emotional blackmail to more severe consequences.

So, let's dive into the strategies to safeguard yourself from potential backlash:

Anticipate, Don't Speculate

The first step is to recognize that there might be an adverse reaction. A toxic partner thrives on control; they might lash out when they sense they're losing it. Preparing is not about fearing the worst but equipping yourself for any outcome.

Leave a Paper Trail

It might sound tedious, but it's essential. Maintain a record of any form of abuse – messages, emails, or even voice recordings. It's about holding them accountable and having tangible proof if you need to involve authorities.

Legal Eagles on Your Side

Informing the police or taking legal steps might seem intimidating, but sometimes it's necessary, especially if there's a history of physical abuse. Many places offer free legal aid for such situations. It's not about seeking revenge; it's about ensuring your safety.

Go-bags are Not Just for Movies

Having a 'go-bag' is a practical step. This bag should have essentials like important documents, a set of clothes, some cash, medications, and emergency contact numbers. Place it somewhere accessible, so if you ever need to leave in haste, you won't be scrambling.

Have Your Refuge

Identify a safe space. It could be a friend's house, a relative's place, or even a shelter. This is your sanctuary, where you can breathe, regroup, and heal without the looming shadow of the past.

Stay Connected

Ensure a few trusted souls know about your situation. It's not just for emotional support; they can check in on you, be a point of contact, and even help if needed.

I recall when Alexis came for her session, her face glowing with a newfound strength. She told me about the steps she took, the help she got, and the new life she was building. She chuckled, saying, "The storm might've drenched me, but now, I've got a pretty solid umbrella."

Your journey might be filled with puddles, rain, and sometimes a thunderstorm, but with the proper preparation, you can dance in the rain and emerge stronger, drier, and more resilient than before. After all, every storm runs out of rain, right?

I met a bright-eyed woman named Lara in my office. She wore her heart on her sleeve and had a vivacity that was hard to miss. As she opened up, she mentioned she'd finally mustered the strength to distance herself from a toxic relationship. But now, the emotional backlash was taking a toll.

I remember thinking, "Ah, the aftermath. The emotional tornado that seems so merciless after you've taken the brave step to distance yourself."

Let's unpack this emotional whirlwind.

THE EMOTIONAL PREPAREDNESS

If there's one thing I've observed over the years, the emotional turbulence after a break from a toxic relationship can sometimes be as challenging as the relationship itself. Why? Because facing backlash often means you're disrupting the toxic equilibrium. You're challenging the status quo. And that is usually a sign that you're on the right track.

The initial reactions of guilt, self-doubt, and even loneliness are common. But they are not permanent.

The Guilt Trips and Emotional Blackmail

You might recognize some of these phrases: "After all I've done for you," "You're breaking our family apart," or "I can't live without you."

While these statements might sting, it's essential to see them for what they are – manipulative tools to regain control.

When faced with guilt trips, my mantra is – reflect, don't absorb. Recognize these manipulations, take a moment, and ask yourself, "Is this guilt mine to carry?" More often than not, it isn't.

Navigating Emotional Blackmail

The underbelly of toxic relationships is often emotional blackmail. It's a cocktail of fear, obligation, and guilt. Remember Lara? She faced threats of self-harm from her partner if she dared to leave. As horrifying as it was, she needed to understand that she wasn't responsible for someone else's choices.

The key is to maintain boundaries. And if the threats escalate, do not hesitate to involve professionals or authorities.

A small tidbit from my practice: I once advised Lara to visualize a shield, reflecting her partner's threats and guilt trips. It might sound whimsical, but visual aids sometimes provide the emotional distance we need.

Empower Yourself

Knowledge is power. Understanding the dynamics of emotional blackmail and recognizing guilt trips gives you a leg up. Equip yourself with tools - books, support groups, therapy sessions, or even joining online forums. Share, learn, and grow from collective wisdom.

As our sessions progressed, Lara gradually transformed. Not overnight, but slowly and surely, she learned to shield herself, deflect, and hold her ground.

In the end, breaking free isn't just about physical distance. It's also about untangling those emotional webs. And as you stride forward, remember you're not alone. The journey might seem daunting, but with each step, you're moving closer to the freedom and peace you deserve. You've got this!

RECLAIMING THE SELF: MIRANDA AND GAIL'S STORIES

Years back, a fresh-faced Miranda walked into my office. As an ICU nurse, she radiated a mixture of determination and vulnerability. Sighing, she said, " I don't know who I've become." Her story was a classic case of isolation – a tool many toxic partners employ. By cutting her off from her lifeline of family and friends, her fiancée, Jeffrey, ensured Miranda's emotional dependence on him intensified. The vision of her wedding day, which should be joyous, was shadowed by a void filled with faceless guests and silent disapproval.

Miranda's struggle was real and echoed in many of my sessions. She was in love. But love should be the wind beneath your wings, not shackles that weigh you down.

On the other hand, Gail, a vivacious event planner, found her once-booming voice muted over time. Gail painted a vivid picture of herself, likening her position to that of a mouse cornered, awaiting its fate at the jaws of a snake. While her choice of words was poetic, the reality was far from it. Her everyday life was a dance on eggshells, with the shadow of Jeremy's unpredictable outbursts looming large.

Relating these stories to the journey of breaking free, the first step lies in recognition. Miranda and Gail needed to understand that love and fear shouldn't reside in the same space. For Miranda, the thought of marrying Jeffrey should be one of bliss, not loneliness. For Gail, coming home should evoke feelings of safety and comfort, not terror.

The true essence of love is freedom – the freedom to be yourself, to nurture relationships outside of your romantic partnership, and to live without the dark cloud of unpredictability hanging overhead.

Reclaiming oneself is not just about creating physical distance from toxicity but also an emotional and psychological reclamation. It's about reminiscing who you were before the relationship took a toll on your identity and rebuilding that self.

One evening, while Miranda was gazing at the sunset, she had a moment of epiphany. She realized she didn't just miss her friends; she missed herself – the laughter, the joy, the freedom. Gail, on the other hand, joined a support group. Listening to similar experiences, she realized she deserved a life free from constant fear.

While the path to breaking free isn't easy and is filled with moments of self-doubt, it is also sprinkled with rediscovery, strength, and eventual peace. Remember, your journey is your own, and no two paths look alike. What's crucial is to take that first step, even with a shaky foot, towards reclaiming your true self.

Over the years, I've noticed something fascinating. There's a palpable glow in individuals who love them-selves, a radiant energy that attracts positive vibes and genuine connections. Remember when you wore that outfit that made you feel "on top of the world"? The confidence and assurance with which you carried your-self? Imagine feeling that way about your very essence, your soul.

There's a phrase I've grown fond of: "We accept the love we think we deserve." How much love do you believe you deserve? If your answer is limitless, then you're on the right track. If not, don't fret; recognizing that is the first step to transformation.

I remember having a chat with a vibrant woman named Lily. She had been through a whirlwind of toxic relationships, constantly jumping from one to the next, thinking she was the problem. But during our talks, she had a lightbulb moment. She realized that she had been pouring from an empty cup. She sought validation and love from others when she hadn't truly loved herself. Once Lily embarked on her journey of self-love, everything shifted. Relationships, both romantic and platonic, became more fulfilling. She stopped settling for anything less than she deserved.

I want to leave you with this thought: *Love yourself.* It sounds cliché, and I've certainly advised many people the same, but that's because it's that transformative. Loving yourself isn't vanity; it's sanity.

7

AFTER THE RAIN – THE RAINBOW OF SELF-LOVE

"If you don't love yourself, nobody will. Not only that, you won't be good at loving anyone else. Loving starts with the self."

— **WAYNE DYER**

There's an unmistakable beauty in the aftermath of a storm. The air feels fresher, and the world, though scarred, stands resilient and ready to begin anew. Much like nature, a rebirth awaits us after the turbulent waves of a toxic relationship recede. But to embrace this new beginning, we must first understand the pain, the lessons, and the scars that have shaped us.

I remember counseling a woman named Julia. She came to me, heart heavy and spirit dampened, after ending a relationship that had drained her essence. Julia's story might sound all too familiar to some of you. She shared how she had lost her identity, molding herself into someone she wasn't just to please another. The weight of compromise, sacrifice, and heartache had burdened her soul. But as our sessions progressed, I saw her shift from a woman full of regret to someone with renewed purpose. Julia didn't just survive the storm; she became its master, using the lessons to shape a brighter, more vibrant self.

Toxic relationships, as painful as they are, gift us insights. They show us our strengths and vulnerabilities, and most importantly, they teach us the actual value of self-love.

THE PATH TO REBUILDING ONESELF POST-TOXIC RELATIONSHIP

There's an unparalleled clarity that storms bring. As fierce winds blow and raindrops pound the earth, the sky gradually clears up, revealing a canvas of azure blue. In the same vein, while the end of a toxic relationship might seem like an insurmountable storm, it's often a precursor to a clearer understanding of oneself.

Thirty years in therapy have shown me countless individuals who, after navigating a tumultuous relationship, feel trudging through a never-ending storm. But with time and the proper steps, they found their rainbow.

1. **Allow Yourself to Mourn:** You're not just grieving the relationship but the dreams, promises, and futures you both once envisioned. I recall a couple of years back when a patient admitted to me, "I don't just miss him; I miss the 'us' we once were." Mourning isn't a sign of weakness; it's an essential part of the healing process.

2. **Reconnect with Yourself:** It's easy to lose oneself in the whirlwind of another person's needs, desires, and demands. Take this time to rediscover who you truly are. Whether it's rekindling a long-lost hobby or simply waking up without an alarm, savor those moments. Just last summer, a dear client took a solo trip post-breakup, sharing, "I found pieces of myself in places I never even knew I left them."

3. **Reinforce Boundaries:** This isn't just about setting limits with others but also establishing boundaries for yourself. Recognize and honor your worth. I often say, "Teach people how to

treat you," which begins with understanding your value.

4. **Seek Support:** This could be through therapy, reconnecting with loved ones, or joining a support group. During one of my sessions, a gentleman shared, "I always thought I was alone in my pain until I heard another's story that mirrored my own."

5. **Educate Yourself:** The more you learn about toxic dynamics, the more empowered you become in preventing them in the future. Consider reading books, attending workshops, or simply engaging in conversations on the subject.

6. **Rebuild Trust:** Not just in others, but most importantly, in yourself. Remember, every experience, good or bad, sharpens your intuition. When Phoebe, a resilient woman I worked with, started dating again, she mentioned, "This time, I listened to my gut, not just my heart."

7. **Reaffirm Your Worth Daily:** We live in an age where affirmations are seen as trendy Instagram captions, but their power is undeniable. Start each day with a positive thought about yourself. I've had this mantra for years: "I deserve love, just as I am."

As you venture out on this path of rebuilding, remember that growth often requires discomfort. But just as seeds need to be buried to bloom, so do we sometimes need to be submerged in our struggles to rise stronger. So, gear up. Your rainbow awaits, and trust me, after three decades of witnessing transformations, it's brighter than you can even imagine.

Navigating the tumultuous waters of a post-toxic relationship often mirrors the five stages of grief. I've journeyed with countless individuals, witnessing firsthand the emotional roller coaster these stages bring. And so, let's venture together into these stages, understanding that, like any storm, they too shall pass.

1. **Denial:** The mind is a powerful tool, often using denial as its first line of defense. The end of a relationship can be jolting, and it's natural for the mind to shield itself from the pain. "This isn't happening," I'd often hear, or "They'll change; it was just a bad phase." Remember that denial is not deception but a temporary buffer.
2. **Anger:** Once the shock wears off, anger takes the wheel. I often hear, "Why me? It's not fair!" It isn't fair. But this fury, when channeled correctly, can be a powerful catalyst for change.
3. **Bargaining:** The 'what if' and 'if only' stage. We barter with the universe, promising change for

a restored relationship. My heart aches when I hear, "If only I'd done more, been more, we'd still be together." Remember, love should never come with the cost of losing oneself.

4. **Depression:** A profound sense of loss follows. You might feel hollow, floating through life without an anchor. Hallie, a vibrant lady I worked with, once lamented, "The world has its colors, but all I see is gray." But, like every cloudy day, the sun eventually shines, illuminating paths you never knew existed.

5. **Acceptance:** The most liberating of stages. It doesn't mean you're "over it" or the pain has vanished. Instead, it's an acknowledgment of reality and a commitment to moving forward— a testament to human resilience.

I often hear, "If only I could rewind time." But through that darkness, a newfound_appreciation for life's little moments can emerge. Every stage, however over-whelming, shapes us in beautiful, unpredictable ways.

To you, I promise: the storm does pass, and the rainbow at its end is worth every raindrop. Be patient, be gentle with yourself, and always remember healing isn't linear. Embrace each stage, knowing it brings you one step closer to your own personal rainbow.

There's a wise saying: when you find yourself lost in a forest, don't just do something; stand there. As counter-intuitive as that might sound, the essence of this message is about the power of reflection. Over the years, I've emphasized to countless individuals the transformative potential of self-reflection after a challenging life event. And leaving a toxic relationship certainly qualifies as such.

Walking out of a storm doesn't automatically lead one to calm waters. There's this moment, soaked to the bone, where you must wring out the wet, take a deep breath, and chart your new course. This is where self-reflection shines.

In the aftermath of a toxic relationship, you are essentially lost in a figurative forest. And self-reflection is your map.

1. **Understanding what went wrong:** At the heart of this exercise is discernment. It isn't about assigning blame – either to yourself or your ex-partner. Instead, it's about pinpointing patterns, behaviors, or decisions that might've been harmful. So many people ask, "Why do I feel so drained?" That nagging question is understanding the dynamics that were at play in relationships.

2. **Recognizing patterns:** We humans are creatures of habit. Often, we get into relational patterns without realizing it. Self-reflection allows us to connect the dots. It could constantly be seeking validation or choosing partners we can fix. Identifying these patterns is the first step in changing them.

3. **Avoiding future pitfalls:** With self-reflection clarity, we become better equipped to navigate future relationships. Knowing your triggers, understanding your worth, and being clear about your boundaries will ensure you avoid falling into familiar traps.

Now, self-reflection doesn't mean endless rumination or spiraling into negative thoughts. It's a constructive process aimed at growth and forward movement. Think of it as a personalized guidebook, where you're both the author and the reader. Only this time, the adventures you write for yourself will be healthier, happier, and filled with genuine self-love.

A few years back, a dear friend gifted me a beautiful journal, its pages crisp and inviting. I began to fill it with my reflections and, in doing so, uncovered patterns, dreams, and desires I'd long buried. I hope you, too, find the courage to turn inward, pen down your thoughts, and allow the cathartic power of self-reflection to guide your next chapter.

Ah, love! It's the stuff of movies, songs, and endless stories that bring us together in a shared experience. Yet, it's a fascinating truth that the most vital relationship one can have is often the most overlooked: the relationship with oneself.

You see, after the storm of a toxic relationship, there's a subtle societal pressure, sometimes even self-imposed, to 'bounce back' to find someone new to fill that void. And here's where I urge a gentle pause, a soft touch of the brakes.

I once worked with a lovely woman named Marta. Having come out of a 15-year tumultuous marriage, she was eager, almost in a hurry, to find someone new. But, like a good wine or a blooming flower, certain things cannot be hurried. They need time, care, and nurturing.

Marta came to our session one afternoon with an "aha" moment. She said, "You know, I've realized I've been dating for over two decades, and in all this time, I never really dated... myself." That was her lightbulb moment. She realized she'd been seeking external validation while missing the immense love she could offer herself.

Let me share something with you. The process of rebuilding isn't about preparing for another romantic relationship. No, it's about rekindling a passionate, compassionate, and unconditional love affair with yourself. It's about recognizing your worth, valuing your needs, and understanding that your happiness isn't a secondary concern—it's paramount.

So, what does 'dating yourself' look like?

1. **Discovering Your Interests:** Dive into things that bring you joy. Be it painting, dancing, hiking, or sitting in a quiet café with a book. Revel in these moments that are solely for you.

2. **Setting Boundaries:** Early in my career, I overbooked my calendar, trying to be there for everyone, only to feel utterly drained. Learn from my early therapist days and say 'no' when necessary.

3. **Self-Care:** Not the commercialized spa-day type (unless that's what you're into), but the kind that nourishes your soul. Meditate, write, listen to music, or take a long, leisurely bath.

4. **Therapy and Self-Help:** Remember, seeking help isn't a sign of weakness. It's an act of courage. Whether through books, workshops, or one-on-one sessions, find what supports your growth.

5. **Laugh:** Let's remember this one! The world can seem heavy, but laughter remains a universal healer. Find humor in the little things, watch a comedy, or share a joke with a friend.

Talking about Marta, her transformation was nothing short of awe-inspiring. Instead of jumping into another relationship, she took a sabbatical, traveled, learned pottery, and, most importantly, fell in love with herself. Now, I'm not suggesting everyone take such drastic measures. Still, Marta's journey underscores a pivotal point: in pursuing love, don't forget the magnificent, beautiful, resilient being that is YOU because you are a love story in yourself.

STRATEGIES FOR SELF-LOVE

Navigating the aftermath of a toxic relationship is like traversing through a dense forest. You might feel disoriented and yearn for a clear path. While your experiences are deeply personal and unique, here are some tried-and-true strategies I've seen work wonders. Remember, this is your journey, and the tools I suggest are here to serve you, so take what resonates and leave the rest.

1.The Power of Therapy: In the healing journey, therapy often acts as the North Star. There are various forms to consider:

- **Toxic Relationship Counseling**: A specialized area that addresses the intricate dynamics you've faced. It helps unravel patterns, heal wounds, and equip you with strategies to avoid similar relationships in the future.
- **Cognitive Behavioral Therapy (CBT)**: Effective for changing negative thought patterns and behaviors. Imagine CBT as that friend who challenges your self-deprecating thoughts with logic.
- **Trauma Counseling**: If your relationship was particularly abusive, trauma counseling goes deep, addressing the painful memories and helping you release them.

2. Meditation: If I had a penny for every time I recommended this to my clients. Meditation fosters a connection with oneself. It allows a quiet moment to reflect and cultivate inner peace. The effects can be profound, even for just 5 minutes a day.

3. Journaling: There's something therapeutic about pouring your feelings onto paper. Write without judgment. Let it be raw, honest, and unfiltered. A couple of years ago, I had a client who discovered her love for poetry through journaling. She'd weave her emotions into verses, transforming her pain into art.

4. Art Therapy: Speaking of art, it's not just for the 'creatives' out there. Doodle, paint, sculpt, or even indulge in adult coloring books. It's a way to express emotions that words sometimes fail to capture.

5. Cultivating Self-Love Rituals: Small daily habits can be potent. Treat yourself to a favorite meal, indulge in a skincare routine, or set aside a 'me-time' daily. Remember, self-love isn't just bubble baths and chocolates; it's also setting boundaries and prioritizing your well-being.

6. Educate Yourself: There's strength in knowledge. Read up on the signs of a healthy relationship, understand the nuances of emotional manipulation, and familiarize yourself with what a balanced partnership feels like. The more you know, the better equipped you'll be moving forward.

Let me share a short story. In the late '90s, I had a client named Beth, a vibrant young lady who'd faced a string of manipulative relationships. She came to me defeated, her spark nearly extinguished. As we explored these strategies together, Beth had a transformation. It wasn't overnight, but I watched as she rekindled her relationship with herself over time. She took up pottery, journaled ferociously, and even led group meditation sessions. Her journey was a testament to the power of self-love.

There isn't a one-size-fits-all approach. Healing is deeply personal. But remember this: In the vast forest of life, while the trees and paths may be uncertain, the love and care you give yourself will be the compass guiding you home. And believe me, the journey back to oneself is the most beautiful journey you'll ever embark on.

I've had the privilege of witnessing countless individuals find their way back to themselves. Each journey has been unique, yet the universal need for acceptance, love, and respect underscores every story. This desire often gets clouded, especially after a toxic relationship.

I remember Tami, a brilliant writer who once came to me. A mother of two, she had just ended a tumultuous 15-year marriage. "I feel like I've been running a marathon with weights on," she confessed. What stood out to me about Tami wasn't her pain but her incredible resilience and hope.

And that's the message I want to leave you with. The past may have been stormy, but the skies ahead are clear and inviting. As you rebuild yourself, don't just aim to heal from the toxicity but strive to create a sanc-tuary of love for yourself. A space where respect isn't a luxury but a given. Where understanding isn't begged for but freely offered.

Whether you decide to venture into another relation-ship or take time to cultivate the one with yourself, remember this: love should be an uplifting song, not a binding chain. Surround yourself with those who harmonize with your tune, not those who drown it out.

It's only natural to have scars after being in the storms for so long, but let them not be a mark of pain but badges of survival and resilience. The next chapter of your life is unwritten and in your hands. When you pick up that pen, write with love, respect, and a deep understanding of your worth.

No matter where the road takes you next, remember the essence of what love should be. Because when love is true and pure, it's not just an emotion; it's a force that can heal, rejuvenate, and inspire. Embrace that truth, and let it guide you to the love story you truly deserve. And as Tami told me once, a year into her healing jour-ney, "The best love story I ever wrote was the one with myself." So go on, pen down your masterpiece.

8

ON TO BRIGHTER DAYS

"A healthy relationship doesn't drag you down. It inspires you to be better."

— MANDY HALE

As the sun rises to paint the horizon with warm hues, a similar awakening happens within our souls. The dawn of realization is when we understand our worth and deserve love and respect. After a stormy night, brighter days always follow. And just like that, after weathering the storm of a toxic relationship, you, too, are heading to brighter days.

Over the years, I've sat across many tear-filled eyes, seeking guidance on how to move forward. They often ask, "Is there hope for me? Can I ever find a healthy relationship?" And I'd tell them a story I once heard.

A woman named Gillian walked into my office. Having escaped an emotionally draining relationship, she carried the burden of her past like a backpack filled with bricks. Every step she took towards a new relationship was heavy, filled with fear and skepticism.

But, much like you, Gillian had a spirit that refused to be dimmed. Together, we embarked on a journey of rediscovering love. And here's the thing: love wasn't hiding under a rock or locked behind a closed door. It was right there, within her, waiting to be embraced.

So, as we proceed, let's keep one thing crystal clear: Love, in its purest form, should never feel like a prison. It should feel like wings. Let's walk together on this path and discover what true love looks and feels like. Let's break down the walls and learn how to build bridges toward healthier, fulfilling relationships because you are worth every ounce of genuine love and happiness. And it's time to claim it.

WHAT A BALANCED, RESPECTFUL RELATIONSHIP LOOKS LIKE

Let me paint a picture for you. Two people standing on opposite banks of a river. Both yearn to be together, but the waters are rapid, tumultuous, and downright treacherous. That river represents the toxicity we've been talking about. Now, let's change the scene. Instead of two individuals looking longingly from afar, they're now standing together on a bridge that spans the river safely above the turbulent waters. This bridge is built on mutual respect, trust, understanding, and growth. It's sturdy, reliable, and allows them to meet halfway.

HEALTHY RELATIONSHIPS ARE LIKE BRIDGES

I've seen my share of bridges – some sturdy, others rickety. Over three decades, I've had the privilege to counsel countless individuals, helping them identify the pillars that hold relationships firm against the toughest storms.

1. **Mutual Respect**: If love is the foundation of a relationship, respect is its cornerstone. It's an understanding that the person across from you has their thoughts, feelings, and dreams, which

deserve as much consideration as yours. About 15 years ago, Maureen shared with me her frustrations. Her partner constantly belittled her career aspirations. The moment she decided to seek a relationship where her dreams were celebrated, not mocked, was the day her life transformed.

2. **Trust** is that unwavering faith that your partner will catch you when you fall. It's the belief that your vulnerabilities won't be used as ammunition during disagreements. I recall a gentleman named Ethan, who, despite having faced betrayal in the past, learned that genuine trust in a partner is the glue that binds two souls.

3. **Understanding**: Have you ever had a moment where you felt truly *seen* by someone? That's the magic of understanding. It's looking past the words to comprehend the emotions and feelings beneath. Remember, it's not about agreeing on everything but embracing the differences.

4. **Growth**: A blooming relationship isn't static. Just as we evolve as individuals, our relationships should mature. Growth means facing challenges hand in hand, celebrating

each other's successes, and constantly working towards being better partners.

All relationships have their fair share of challenges. The difference in a healthy relationship is how these challenges are faced. They become opportunities, not obstructions.

I remember a woman named Mia used a plant as an analogy. She said it represented her relationship. Some days, it flourished, and some days, it wilted a bit. But she and her partner always made sure to nurture it back to health because, to them, it was a symbol of their shared growth. I found it a profoundly beautiful analogy.

Remember, building and maintaining such a bridge takes time. It takes time, patience, and consistent effort. It might also mean seeking help, attending couples therapy, or reading books (wink). But the view from the middle of the bridge, hand in hand with someone who genuinely loves and respects you, is worth every ounce of effort.

In our journey together, as we pave the path to brighter days, remember that you deserve a safe, comforting, and joyous relationship. A bridge above stormy waters, leading you both to a horizon filled with promise.

ELEMENTS OF A BALANCED RELATIONSHIP

In the vibrant tapestry of relationships, every stitch and every color tells a story. Some stories resonate with warmth and tenderness, while others are fraught with tension. Having a well-balanced relationship is like possessing a treasure many seek but few indeed find. I want you to know it's attainable, and I'm here to guide you towards it.

Remember when, about 20 years ago, I had a young couple in my office? Clara would always complete Ben's sentences, thinking she knew best. One day, Ben whispered, "I just want to be heard." That was their turning point. Here's what I've gleaned over the years about what a balanced, respectful relationship truly embodies:

1. **Open Communication**: If a relationship were a house, communication would be its foundation. It's more than just talking; it's about genuinely listening. Like with Clara and Ben, it's vital to let your partner express themselves without interruptions or assumptions. And, occasionally, it's checking in with a simple, "How was your day?"

2. **Mutual Respect**: I recall an old adage, "Treat others how you want to be treated." It's as simple and as profound as that. Recognize and

honor the boundaries, feelings, and aspirations of each other.

3. **Equality**: Once, during a group therapy session, a participant quipped, "We're not on the same page; we're not even in the same book!" Every partner should have an equal say and equally invest in decisions, challenges, and responsibilities. It's not about 50-50, but 100-100.

4. **Trust**: Oh, the stories I could tell about broken and mended trusts. Trust is the silent engine that powers relationships. It's not just about fidelity; it's about believing your partner has your best interests at heart and won't hurt or deceive you.

5. **Understanding**: It's that warm blanket on a cold winter's day. It's striving to understand the why behind the what. The most beautiful example was Liza, who took the time to learn sign language when her partner, John, started losing his hearing. Love wasn't just in grand gestures but in understanding his silent world.

I often joke with my friends that my husband and I have a 'psychic connection.' But it's not magic; it's years of practicing these elements, choosing each day to improve, communicating more openly, and understanding more deeply. It's recognizing that even in silence, a lot can be communicated.

Like any beautiful journey, your relationship will have its share of flat tires and unexpected rain. Yet, with these elements as your compass, you can always find your way back. It won't always be easy, but oh, the vistas you'll see and the tales you'll have to tell! So, shall we continue on this journey to brighter days together?

RED FLAGS VS. GREEN FLAGS IN BUDDING RELATIONSHIPS

Ah, the thrill of new love! Those delightful butterflies in the stomach, late-night chats, and lingering daydreams. I've seen the euphoria of fresh romance countless times in my office. But, as the infatuation stage starts to wane, it's important to discern if the relationship is on a healthy trajectory or if there are some concerning signs.

A client told me, "I ignored the red flags because I wanted them to like me." Let's unpack those 'red flags.'

Red Flags:

1. **Excessive Jealousy**: It's like that overly clingy friend who doesn't like you having other friends. A partner who is constantly suspicious

or overprotective can stifle the very essence of a relationship.

2. **Constant Invalidation**: Remember Marissa, whom I mentioned in earlier sessions? She constantly heard phrases like, "You're overreacting" or "You're too sensitive." These aren't words of endearment; they're tools of manipulation.

3. **Attempts to Control**: If you find your wardrobe, friendships, or life choices under the scanner, it's not a protective gesture; it's controlling. It's like being a bird in a cage, beautiful but not free.

4. **Never Taking Responsibility**: Have you ever met someone who never admits they're wrong? It's always the traffic's fault, the weather, or even the neighbor's cat, but never theirs.

5. **Disrespect Towards Boundaries**: Like when someone eats your secret stash of chocolates without asking. In relationships, it's more complex but just as essential.

Now, let's shift our focus. In between the clouds, there are always silver linings. While 'red flags' are warning signs, 'green flags' are indicators that you're on a promising path.

Green Flags:

1. **Active Listening**: Instead of waiting for their turn to speak, they genuinely hear you out. It's like when you want to share the worst part of your day, and they're all ears.
2. **Consistent Respect**: Not just during the honeymoon phase, but even when the going gets tough.
3. **Encouraging Independence**: A relationship isn't about losing oneself; it's about growing together. When they celebrate your individuality, it's a bright green flag.
4. **Open, Honest Communication**: They'd discuss rather than dismiss issues. It's like having a partner for a dance, where both lead and follow, and the rhythm flows.
5. **Shared Values**: It's not about liking the same pizza toppings but more about having shared life goals, mutual respect for individuality, and common core values.

I asked a couple who was celebrating their 50th wedding anniversary. When asked about their secret, the old gentleman winked and said, "We always knew which flags to hoist and which to lower."

Deciphering the flags in your relationship is crucial. Like in any adventure, whether at sea or in love, knowing the signs helps navigate the journey. Here's to recognizing the flags and steering toward brighter days!

I recalled a couple I once counseled. Mark and Judi were like fire and water - passionate, yet cooling each other's tempers. They taught me a valuable lesson about the nuances of love. Relationships aren't just black and white; they're a canvas painted with red and green flags. Let's contrast these flags to understand the dance of love better.

1. **Jealousy (Red) vs. Trust and Confidence (Green)** In the early days of Mark and Judi's relationship, Mark often felt insecure when Judi spent time with her male friends. His jealousy (a red flag) became evident. Over time, with open communication, Mark learned to trust Judi. He developed confidence (a green flag) in their bond, understanding that Judi's friendships didn't threaten their relationship.

2. **Invalidation (Red) vs. Active Listening and Validation (Green)** Remember Clara, who used to be told she was "too emotional"? That's invalidation. On the flip side, during a session, Judi expressed her frustrations. Instead of dismissing her, Mark actively listened and

validated her feelings. Their relationship flourished because they felt seen and heard.

3. **Control (Red) vs. Encouraging Independence (Green)** Judi once shared a story about an ex who'd dictate what she could wear. Such control is a glaring red flag. In contrast, when Mark encouraged Judi to take that solo art trip to Italy, it showed he respected and encouraged her independence. A vibrant green flag, indeed!

4. **Avoiding Responsibility (Red) vs. Accountability (Green)** I once met a young lady who said her partner blamed everyone and everything for his mistakes. We want accountability, the willingness to own up to one's actions. After one heated argument, Mark took a deep breath, admitted his mistake, and they both moved forward.

5. **Disregarding Boundaries (Red) vs. Mutual Respect for Limits (Green)** Imagine having a diary that someone reads without your permission. That's how Judi felt when her boundaries were crossed in past relationships. With Mark, they had an unwritten code of respecting each other's limits, whether it was personal space or not discussing specific past traumas.

In my years of counseling, I've seen countless stormy and serene relationships. But the ones that stood out had a balance, a dance between acknowledging the red flags and celebrating the green ones.

A card landed on my desk years ago with a picturesque view of the Amalfi Coast. It was from Judi, sipping wine and painting, her heart content. She wrote, "We're learning to paint our canvas with more green flags each day." And that is what I hope for you - a canvas that radiates hope, love, and a lot of green.

Over the years, I've been a silent witness to tales of both joy and despair. But today, let's delve into an area where many have stumbled, only to emerge stronger: discerning the green flags from the red in the realm of love.

Jealousy vs. Trust and Confidence

I remember Carla, a vibrant woman with sparkling eyes. Her partner's jealousy shadowed her every move. The feeling of being perpetually monitored was suffocating. On the other hand, it was evident when Shelly recounted how her partner, David, celebrated her successes without envy. Trust and confidence are the cornerstones of love, a brilliant green flag waving in the breeze.

Invalidation vs. Active Listening and Validation

Once, a young man named Max confided that his partner often dismissed his feelings, saying he was "overreacting." Ah, the sting of invalidation! But then there's Emma, whose partner would lean in, listen, and validate her feelings, even if they didn't always understand them. Recognizing and cherishing those green flag moments can bring so much solace.

Control vs. Encouraging Independence

Years ago, I met Lina, who was constantly second-guessing herself because her partner insisted on making every decision for her. The red flag of control can be subtle yet insidious. In contrast, consider Mike, who cheered when his wife, Janet, decided to take a solo trip to explore her passion for photography. Their relationship thrived on mutual respect and the encouragement of independence - a bright green flag.

Avoiding Responsibility vs. Accountability

I chuckled when recalling Tim, who had an amusing knack for attributing his forgotten anniversaries to "aliens meddling with his memory." But jokes aside, dodging responsibility is a significant red flag. When we encounter someone who owns their actions and apologizes sincerely, we're in the comforting shade of a green flag.

Disregarding Boundaries vs. Mutual Respect for Limits

Sophie once tearfully shared how her partner read her journal, a clear invasion of her privacy. Red flag alert! But there's hope. I've seen couples set boundaries about personal space or topics off-limits and respect them. It's a green flag that assures both partners feel safe and valued.

Navigating relationships can feel like treading through a dense forest with green canopies and looming thorns. Always remember to be vigilant. While spotting the red flags is essential, it's equally crucial to celebrate the green ones.

And when you feel lost, imagine sitting with me in my therapy room discussing those flags. You're not alone on this journey. Here's to brighter days and healthier relationships sprinkled generously with those reassuring green flags!

STEPS TO ENSURE TOXIC PATTERNS DON'T RESURFACE IN FUTURE RELATIONSHIPS

I remember sitting in my office one warm afternoon when Lucy, a bubbly woman in her late thirties, came in. She had a twinkle in her eyes but a certain heaviness in her heart. "I'm scared," she admitted. "I've met someone new and don't want to repeat the same toxic patterns." We talked about the clear and concise roadmap. And today, I share the same with you.

1. The Power of Self-reflection and Awareness

Like Lucy, many of you have walked out of a toxic relationship, but the ghosts of the past keep haunting you. One of the first steps in ensuring they don't sneak into your future relationships is self-awareness. Set aside regular "Me Time." Dive deep into understanding yourself, your triggers, and your patterns.

Remember when you found that odd sock behind the washing machine? It had been missing for ages! Self-reflection is a bit like that. You discover emotions and triggers you didn't know were lurking in the shadows.

2. Journaling: Your Personal Beacon

If I had a penny for every time someone told me journaling changed their life, I'd be... well, let's say I'd have a lot of pennies. But it's no jest. Journaling helps you recognize patterns. When Lucy started writing down her feelings, she noticed she felt anxious every time her partner was late. Delving deeper, she realized it was an old wound from her previous relationship, where her partner would often lie about his whereabouts.

3. Embrace Continuous Learning

Knowledge is transformative. Websites, podcasts, and books can offer insights into self-reflection and its benefits. Remember, you're not just reading for the sake of it. These resources help you recognize and break patterns, paving the way for healthier relationships.

4. Lean on Your Support System

Having friends or therapists to talk to is like having a GPS for your emotions. They might see things you're too close to notice. They can alert you when you're drifting into old patterns.

5. Celebrate the Small Wins

Have you caught yourself before reacting in an old, toxic way? Pat yourself on the back because you recognized and communicated a boundary. Get that slice of cheesecake you've been eyeing!

6. Remember, it's Okay to Seek Help.

A few months into her new relationship, Lucy returned, not with problems, but to share her happiness and ensure she was on the right track. It's always okay to ask for guidance.

To sum it up, the road ahead seems daunting. But as Lucy discovered, with the right tools and self-awareness, you can ensure those old toxic patterns become a thing of the past. Let's embark on this journey, one step at a time, to a future filled with healthier, brighter relationships.

I recall when Kathy, a woman of grace and resilience, confided in me about her journey through tumultuous relationships. As she spoke, her vulnerability was evident. "I've always felt like I was walking on eggshells," she murmured. "But now, I want to be in charge of my happiness." Kathy's words resonated deeply, as I had heard similar sentiments from countless individuals over the years. They all sought one essential element: boundaries.

UNDERSTANDING BOUNDARIES: THE UNSUNG HEROES OF RELATIONSHIPS

Imagine going on a theme park ride without any safety barriers. Sounds chaotic and dangerous, right? That's what a relationship without boundaries looks like. Boundaries are your safety barriers that define what's okay and what's not in a relationship.

Draw Your Line in the Sand

Start by understanding your limits. What are you comfortable with? What makes your heart race with anxiety? These questions aren't just reflective exercises; they are your first step in defining your boundaries.

Here's a humorous yet poignant anecdote. Years ago, when I was just dipping my toes into relationships, I dated someone with a penchant for surprise visits. One day, they decided to pop in while I was in my pajamas, hair resembling a bird's nest, belting out to an old 80s ballad. Embarrassing? Oh, absolutely. A learning experience? Most definitely. I realized I needed my space and boundaries, even from someone I cared about.

Communicate, Don't Dictate

There's an art to setting boundaries. It's not about listing demands or rules. Instead, it's about communicating what you need to feel safe, respected, and loved. A simple phrase like, "I value our time together, but I also need time for myself" can go a long way.

Consistency is Key

Setting boundaries is one thing, but maintaining them is another ball game altogether. Remember, it's okay to remind your partner if they accidentally overstep. It's all part of the growth journey.

Embrace the Change

Boundaries might initially feel restrictive, especially if you need to get used to having them. But over time,

186 | TERRI PENDLETON, LMHC

you'll see that they pave the way for deeper connection and understanding.

Numerous resources exist if you're craving a deeper dive into this topic. For instance, Eugene Therapy and Positive Psychology have comprehensive guides on setting and maintaining boundaries. They're treasure troves of wisdom, so do give them a glance.

Boundaries aren't just walls but gateways to healthier, happier relationships. With her newfound understanding, Kathy blossomed in her relationships, and I am confident that with these tools at your disposal, you, too, can steer your ship toward brighter days. And always remember, it's okay to sing your heart out in your pajamas; just set a boundary for unexpected visitors!

Ah, therapy! It's one of those hushed words we often whisper in the safe confinements of trusted circles. But why? Thirty years ago, in the early stages of my career, the stigma around seeking therapy was palpable. Fast forward to now, the world has shifted, and therapy is no longer an "unspoken" realm but a celebrated space of healing and discovery.

A few years back, I remember sitting on my worn couch that had heard stories of countless brave individuals. A young woman named Lauren came in. She had these bright eyes that bore the weight of many suppressed tears. She said, "It's like I have this internal magnet that keeps drawing me to the same type of toxic partners, and I can't figure out why!" It echoed a sentiment I've encountered numerous times, leading us to our next vital step: therapy.

Revisiting Chapter 7: We previously delved deep into understanding the intricacies of a balanced relationship. And while awareness is a mighty tool, sometimes, unearthing and dismantling deep-seated patterns require professional guidance.

Why Therapy?

If our minds were gardens, some patches might become overgrown, cluttered, or even infested over time. Therapy, in its essence, is like a dedicated gardener guiding you, helping you recognize those patches, and teaching you the art of tending to them. It's not about "fixing" you; it's about journeying together toward understanding, healing, and growth.

You might wonder, "Why can't I just talk to my friends or family?" Well, imagine you've sprained your ankle. Your dear ones might offer love and sympathy, maybe even an anecdote or two about their sprains. But wouldn't you seek a doctor for proper care? Similarly, therapists are trained to navigate the complexities of the human mind.

How Does It Help?

Therapy provides you with tools to:

1. Recognize toxic patterns: Often, we are blind to our habits, especially if they've been ingrained since childhood.
2. Understand the 'why': It delves deep into the root causes, enabling you to understand why you might be drawn to particular dynamics.
3. Equip yourself with coping mechanisms, strategies, and the strength to make healthier choices.

I remember Lauren's journey. It was a series of ups and downs, but with every session, she grew, not just in understanding but in strength and self-worth. By the end, she recognized her patterns and had the tools to ensure they didn't bind her.

Stepping into therapy can feel like standing at the edge of an unknown ocean, but remember, every wave and tide is a step towards a brighter, healthier you. As we continue our journey in this book, always remember that seeking help is not a sign of weakness but a testament to your strength. And just between you and me, the best gardeners always know when to seek an expert's touch.

Around two decades ago, I found myself in a coffee shop chatting with an old friend, Roberta. She animatedly talked about her latest hiking adventure, but I noticed an underlying tension. In a quiet moment, she confessed, "Every time I share my feelings with Marco, it feels like tossing messages into a vast sea, hoping they'd wash ashore." This analogy struck a chord.

Open Communication:

If relationships were like gardens (yes, I love gardening metaphors!), open communication would be the sunlight. Without it, everything withers. But with it? Ah, the blossoms and the hues! Regularly checking in with your partner is like ensuring that every corner of your garden receives its fair share of light.

In my years of practice, the underlying cause of many relationship woes has been a lack of open communication. It's a learned skill, yes, but immensely rewarding. Address concerns when they are saplings, not when they've grown into tangled bushes. After all, it's easier to untie a single knot than an entire web.

Remember that one vacation when your baggage got delayed, and you were left without your belongings in a foreign land? Unclear communication in a relationship feels eerily similar. Your emotional baggage doesn't reach its destination, leaving you feeling stranded and unheard.

Practice Self-care:

Let's dive back into Chapter 7 for a moment. Remember when we discussed the significance of caring for oneself in a relationship? It's paramount! Imagine being on an airplane; you're always instructed to put on your oxygen mask first before helping others. Why? Because when you're taken care of, you can care for others better.

Your relationship isn't just about seeking validation from your partner; it's also about validating yourself. Treat yourself with kindness, go for that spa day, read that book, or even indulge in that occasional chocolate soufflé (oh, how it melts just right!).

Roberta and Marco made it a ritual to have a weekly 'talk-it-out' session, phones and TV off. They created a judgment-free zone where they voiced concerns, dreams, and laughable blunders.

They cultivated more than just open communication; they built an environment of trust, understanding, and sheer goofiness.

Relationships are intricate dances of two souls. Ensuring toxic patterns don't resurface is like mastering your dance steps. At times, you might falter, maybe even miss a beat. Remember, the effort, understanding, and the will to move forward hand-in-hand matters most. So, lace up your dancing shoes, and let's waltz on to brighter days!

A few years ago, at a small town fair, I watched a young man trying to win a prize at one of those ring toss games. He was so eager to win the giant teddy bear that he kept rushing his throws, missing every time. An older woman beside him took her time, practiced her aim, and, with patience, managed to get a ring on the peg. She walked away with that teddy bear, leaving the young man in awe. Relationships can be strikingly similar to that ring toss game.

Avoid rushing: I'm not saying love is a carnival game, but the principle stands. In our hurry to find love, or sometimes to escape loneliness, we might rush into relationships. This rush often blinds us to the glaring red flags or the subtle signs of looming toxicity.

Remember when the thrill of a new relationship made everything seem perfect, only for the cracks to appear when the initial excitement faded? Taking things slowly allows you to understand your partner better, to peel off their layers, and to genuinely comprehend if both of you are compatible.

A patient of mine once shared, "I mistook intensity for intimacy. Just because we were moving fast didn't mean we were moving deep." That statement stayed with me.

Stay connected to support systems: During my counseling sessions, I've met countless individuals who've slowly cut ties with their close ones due to their relationship. It's not always intentional; sometimes, it's a gradual drift. However, it's these ties, these connections, that act as our lifeboats in turbulent times.

In Chapter 7, we discussed the significance of support systems. And here, I'd like to reiterate. Your friends, family, or support groups aren't just shoulders to cry on; they are mirrors reflecting perspectives you might miss. They've known you, in some cases, longer than your partner has, and they see things you might overlook in your relationship.

Remember Sarah from a few chapters ago? She confided in her sister about her relationship struggles. Her sister's insight, as an external observer, helped

Sarah recognize patterns she had been oblivious to. This isn't about letting others dictate your love life but allowing those who care about you to share their perspective.

In conclusion, just as you wouldn't buy the first house you see or pick the first dress you try, it's crucial not to rush into relationships or cut off from your tribe. Surround yourself with people who uplift, challenge, and guide you. In the tapestry of life, ensure the threads of patience and connection are woven firmly.

Trust your Gut

Years back, I was sitting across from Sydney, a 40-something-year-old woman with expressive eyes. She looked at me and said, "Every time he raised his voice, every time he made a backhanded comment, a voice inside me said, 'This isn't right.' But I silenced it, thinking it was my paranoia."

Her confession is not an isolated one. Time and time again, people have shared similar sentiments, often regretting not listening to their inner voices. Let me tell you something about that voice.

We often undermine the power of our intuition, brushing it aside for logical reasoning. But that 'gut feeling' isn't baseless. It's your brain's way of picking up irregularities, inconsistencies, or patterns based on past experiences. This intuition becomes even more heightened in the realm of relationships, especially after having encountered toxicity.

I remember standing at the edge of a cliff, taking in the breathtaking view of the sea. I felt the breeze, I saw the waves, but something deep inside me whispered not to get any closer. Our relationship intuition is the same; sometimes, it sees the danger even when the view seems perfect.

So, if a particular behavior or situation triggers memories of past toxic experiences, or even if you can't put a finger on it, something feels off - don't dismiss it. Address it. Ask questions. Seek clarity. And if the alarm bells in your mind persist, remember that they might warn you of a potential rerun of past traumas.

If there's one thing I've observed, people rarely regret listening to their intuition. They mostly regret ignoring it.

So, the next time your internal compass points towards something suspicious in your relationship, recalibrate it. Pause, reflect, and choose your path wisely. Because sometimes, the quietest whispers within us hold the loudest truths.

REFLECTIONS FROM THE STORIES

There's wisdom to be gleaned from each tale, and before we dive into the tools and strategies for healthier relationships, let's revisit the incredible journeys of some brave souls we've discussed.

I remember Jennifer confiding in me, her voice quivering with vulnerability and determination. Wrapped in a relationship where her partner's wallet became her chains, she strived to break free. Her triumph? Rediscovering her sense of self-worth and gradually becoming financially independent. *Lesson*: True love doesn't come with a price tag.

Anthony, a tall and sturdy man, was weighed down not by physical burdens but by the weight of societal expectations. Feeling he had to mask his pain behind a facade of "masculinity," his victory was shattering that mask and embracing his emotions. *Lesson*: True strength lies in authenticity and emotional openness.

Vanessa's story brought tears to my eyes. Bound by the desire to protect her children, she stayed longer than she should have. The twist? Her children were her beacon, urging her towards happiness. *Lesson*: Often, the chains we believe hold us are illusions.

Candace wore rose-tinted glasses, thinking she could nurture change in her partner. Through time and tears, she learned love wasn't about molding someone but cherishing their true self. *Lesson*: We can't sculpt people into our ideal versions; we must appreciate them for who they are.

Abigail's dance with toxicity was cyclical – breaking up, making up, hoping for change. Her triumph was recognizing consistent patterns and understanding that real change isn't intermittent. *Lesson*: Consistency is a language; pay attention to it.

Lisa, Ginger, Yolanda, Susan, Miranda, and Gail each had unique tales but shared threads of resilience and the quest for respect and validation. From them, we understand the value of self-worth and how internal battles often overshadow external ones. *Lesson*: Our inner compass is the best guide, and self-respect is its North Star.

A few years ago, I had a client whose story resonated deeply with these tales. She whispered, "I feel trapped in my life, every corner I turn to." As I urge you now, I encouraged her to understand that we have more power than we often give ourselves credit for.

Each story is a testament to our innate ability to grow, transform, and seek brighter days, even amid storms.

And in their tales lie universal truths. We are all deserving of love, respect, and understanding. Hope isn't just a word; it's a path, an attitude, a belief. And as long as there's hope, there's a way forward. On to brighter days!

CONCLUSION

Through the years in my practice, I've seen countless faces, heard innumerable stories, and felt the weight of many tears. Each tale is unique yet bound by a common thread - the yearning for love that nurtures and understands, not one that belittles and binds.

Our shared journey in these pages wasn't about deciphering a complex algorithm or finding a magical antidote for pain. At its core, it was about recognizing the essence of genuine, empowering love and differentiating it from the shadows of toxicity. Love should be a safe harbor, not a storm you constantly have to weather.

Around seven years ago, a client named Maya walked into my office. She was a living testament to the adage, "What doesn't kill you makes you stronger." Having been in a whirlwind of a toxic relationship for years, she sought change for herself and her beautiful children. Today, Maya is happily remarried, cherishing a bond rooted in mutual respect, understanding, and trust. Her journey wasn't without its hurdles, but her resilience turned her once somber narrative into a glowing testament to the power of self-love and determination.

So, let Maya's story be your beacon. The narratives you've imbibed from this book are tools, keys if you will, to unlock healthier relationships and champion them in every aspect of your life. For every story of despair, there's one of hope waiting to be written.

With all your strengths, vulnerabilities, desires, and dreams, you have an incredible power to shape your relationship destiny and choose love that celebrates rather than diminishes you. Please take the lessons from these pages, apply them to your life, and advocate for healthy love in your circles because everyone deserves a love story free from shadows.

Now, go forth, write your story, and remember: brighter days are not just on the horizon; they're within your grasp.

Over the past three decades, my heart and soul have been deeply interwoven with countless individuals striving for healthier connections. The stories, challenges, tears, and triumphs have all been a testament to the human spirit's ability to find light even in the shadowy corners of love.

I hope the insights shared in this book have served as an illuminating guide and a comforting companion in your journey. Remember that your quest for love should never compromise your essence. And if ever you find yourself at a crossroads, know that the compass to a better tomorrow lies within these pages.

If the guidance within this book has made even the tiniest positive dent in your life, I would deeply appreciate it if you'd take a moment to share a review. Your feedback, experiences, and reflections can light the way for someone else standing at the precipice of change. In the vast sea of narratives, your voice could be the beacon another soul is seeking.

Always remember, life might not come with a manual, but with shared wisdom, experiences, and a sprinkling of tough love, we can pen the most heartening chapters in the book of relationships. You've embarked on this transformative journey, and you're not alone. So, here's to love that empowers, uplifts relationships, and a future filled with understanding and respect.

To brighter days and hopeful tomorrows, cheers! And spread the word, for there's a world out there yearning for tales of redemption and resurgence. Your story might be the lighthouse they've been searching for.

As we conclude, I leave you with a timeless piece that resonates with our shared journey of self-discovery and self-love. Let it serve as a gentle reminder that amidst the tumultuous tides of relationships, the most enduring love is the one we owe to ourselves.

Love After Love – By Derek Walcott

> *The time will come*
> *when, with elation,*
> *you will greet yourself arriving*
> *at your own door, in your own mirror,*
> *and each will smile at the other's welcome,*
> *And say, sit here. Eat.*
> *You will love again the stranger who was*
>   *yourself.*

Give wine. Give bread. Give back your heart
to itself, to the stranger who has loved you
all your life, whom you ignored
for another, who knows you by heart.
Take down the love letters from the bookshelf,
the photographs, the desperate notes,
peel your own image from the mirror.
Sit. Feast on your life.

From Survive to Thrive: Self-care Tips for Healing Beyond Your Toxic Relationship

1. Awareness is the first step towards healing. Take the time to list or reflect on the toxic patterns that you have identified from this book. What are those patterns, and make a list of goals to get out of this toxic relationship.
2. Prioritizing self-care: Practice small acts of self-love daily to strengthen your emotional well-being
3. Reach out to trusted friends, family, or a mental health professional for support. Share your experience and allow yourself to be vulnerable. This will be tough for you who have disconnected from your friends and loved ones, but they still love you and will welcome you back into their lives.
4. Reconnect with hobbies, passions, and activities that bring you joy. You may have forgotten what those were, but what did you love to do or go to? Get out and do them!!
5. Write down some quotes or words of affirmation that empower and uplift you. Repeat them daily to reinforce a positive self-image. Say them over and over again until you believe them!

6. Write down guilt-inducing thoughts on paper, then burn/shred/tear them to symbolize letting go. Having a different train of thought is hard; those negative thoughts will want to creep in. As Zig Ziglar stated, "Don't let negative and toxic people rent space in your head. Raise the rent and kick them out."

7. Write a letter to yourself about what you have been through and what kind of life you truly deserve. Try to be kind and nurturing to yourself instead of beating yourself up.

8. Create a "joy jar" and fill it with notes of happy moments and achievements. When you need a pick-me-up, read the messages.

9. Compile a playlist of empowering songs that boost your spirit during challenging times. Sing them at the top of your lungs!

10. Create a vision board representing your dreams and aspirations for the future. Put it up somewhere so you can see it daily to remind yourself of the life you deserve.

11. Start a gratitude journal where you write one thing you are grateful for each day, and you cannot repeat the same thing during the year. This opens your senses: "What did I see, hear, taste, touch today?" It can be something like "I

took a hot shower, saw a beautiful cloud in the sky, ate a brownie, etc.

12. Set up a self-care routine tailored to your needs, such as exercising, meditating, pampering, participating in a favorite hobby, or getting out in nature.

13. Use a creative outlet like drawing, painting, or writing to express your emotions and experiences related to your toxic relationship.

14. Use healthy distractions when you feel overwhelmed, such as watching a funny movie, listening to music, taking the dog for a walk, etc.

15. Explore EFT (emotional freedom technique) or "tapping" to release emotional blocks and negative energy. This is a great technique and can be used anywhere or anytime.

16. Role reversal exercise- Imagine what you would say to someone else going through your situation. What would you tell them? Write it out if you need to so you can continually say it to yourself.

17. Solo act- go and do something you have never done before, such as going out to eat, a movie, or a museum.

18. Create a bucket list of activities you want when you are free from your toxic relationship.

19. Inner dialogue exercise- write a dialogue between your inner critic and your inner champion that promotes self-compassion and resilience.

20. Values reflection- List your values and assess their alignment with your daily life.

REFERENCES

BetterUp. (n.d.). 11 Toxic Traits to Watch Out For in Yourself and Others. https://www.betterup.com/blog/toxic-traits

Choosing Therapy. (n.d.). Toxic Relationship: How to Know If You're in One and How to Get Out. https://www.choosingtherapy.com/toxic-relationship/

Choudhury, S. (2022, May 17). The End Was Necessary: A Toxic Relationship. YouthKiawaaz. https://www.youthkiawaaz.com/2022/05/the-end-was-necessary-a-toxic-relationship/

Creager, T. (n.d.). A Success Story: She Found Love After Leaving a Toxic Relationship. Todd Creager. https://toddcreager.com/a-success-story-she-found-love-after-leaving-a-toxic-relationship/

Forbes. (2020, May 15). An Average of 80% of Americans have experienced emotional abuse https://www.forbes.com/sites/nazbehashti/2020/05/15/an-average-of-80-Americans-have/experienced-emotional-abuse.

Healthline. (n.d.). What Is a Toxic Relationship and How Do You Leave One? https://www.healthline.com/health/toxic-relationship

Our Mindful Life. (n.d.). 29 Inspiring Quotes to Help You Leave a Toxic Relationship. https://www.ourmindfullife.com/29-inspiring-quotes-help-leave-toxic-relationship/

Sacks, A. (2018, May 8). 12 Signs You May Have an Anxiety Disorder. Time. https://time.com/5274206/toxic-relationship-signs-help/

Smith, M. (2018, May 23). 7 Signs You're in a Toxic Relationship. Women's Health. https://www.womenshealthmag.com/relationships/a19739065/signs-of-toxic-relationship

Stearns, E. (n.d.). How a Toxic Relationship Can Ruin Your Career. Medium. https://medium.com/@BossedUpOrg/how-a-toxic-relationship-can-ruin-your-career-a797d77b97db

Printed in the USA
CPSIA information can be obtained
at www.ICGtesting.com
LVHW020807240324
775321LV00013B/504